Questions and Answers

Q&A

SCIENCE

Single and Double Awards

KEY STAGE 4

Bob McDuell Chief Examiner
Graham Booth Principal Examiner

SERIES EDITOR: BOB McDUELL

Letts EDUCATIONAL

Contents

HOW TO USE THIS BOOK

The aim of the *Questions and Answers* series is to provide you with help to do as well as possible in your exams at GCSE or, in Scotland, at General and Credit levels. This book is based on the idea that an experienced Examiner can give, through examination questions, sample answers and advice, the help students need to secure success and improve their grades.

The *Questions and Answers* series is designed to provide:

- Introductory advice on the different types of question and how to answer them to maximise your marks.
- Information about other skills, apart from the recall of knowledge, that will be tested on examination papers. These are sometimes called **Assessment Objectives** and include communication, problem solving, evaluation and interpretation (see pages 4–5). The *Questions and Answers* series is intended to develop these skills by showing you how marks are allocated.
- **Revision Summaries** to remind you of the topics you will need to have revised in order to answer examination questions.
- Many examples of **examination questions**, arranged by topic, with spaces for you to fill in your answers, just as on an examination paper. Only try the questions once you have revised a topic thoroughly. Read the Revision Summary before attempting the questions to double-check you know the topic. It is best not to consult the answers before trying the questions.
- **Sample answers** to all of the questions.
- **Advice from Examiners**. By using the experience of actual Chief Examiners we are able to give advice on how you can improve your answers and avoid the most common mistakes.

THE IMPORTANCE OF USING QUESTIONS FOR REVISION

Past examination questions play an important part in revising for examinations. However, it is important not to start practising questions too early. Nothing can be more disheartening than trying to do a question which you do not understand because you have not mastered the topic. Therefore, it is important to have studied a topic thoroughly before attempting any questions on it.

How can past examination questions provide a way of preparing for the examination? It is unlikely that any question you try will appear in exactly the same form on the papers you are going to take. However, the examiner is restricted on what can be set because the questions must cover the whole syllabus and test certain Assessment Objectives. The number of totally original questions that can be set on any part of the syllabus is very limited and so similar ideas occur over and over again. It certainly will help you if the question you are trying to answer in an examination is familiar and you know that you have done similar questions before. This is a great boost for your confidence and confidence is what is required for examination success.

Practising examination questions will also highlight gaps in your knowledge and understanding which you can go back and revise more thoroughly. It will also indicate which sorts of questions you can do well.

Attempting past questions will get you used to the type of language used in questions.

Finally, having access to answers, as you do in this book, will enable you to see clearly what is required by the examiner, how best to answer each question, and the amount of detail required. Attention to detail is a key aspect of achieving success at GCSE.

EXAMINATION TECHNIQUE

Success in GCSE examinations comes from proper preparation and a positive attitude to the examination. This book is intended to help you overcome 'examination nerves' which often come from a fear of not being properly prepared. Examination technique is extremely important and certainly affects your performance. Remember the basics:

- Read the questions carefully.
- Make sure that you watch the time carefully and complete the paper. It is no good answering one question well if you spend so long doing it that you do not answer another question at all.
- Read the rubric on the front of the examination paper carefully to make sure you know how many questions to attempt.
- Examination papers usually tell you how many marks are available for each answer. Take notice of this information as the number of marks gives a guide to the importance of the question and often to the amount which you ought to write.
- Check before the end of the examination that you have not missed any pages. Remember to turn over the last page, too.
- Remember to leave time to check through your work carefully.

DIFFERENT TYPES OF EXAMINATION QUESTION

There are different types of examination question which appear on examination papers. Most questions on GCSE Science papers are structured questions.

Structured questions

These are the most common type of question used at GCSE on Science papers. All of the questions in the main part of this book are structured questions. The reason why they are used so widely is that they are so versatile. They can be short, with little opportunity for extended writing; in this form they are suitable for use on Basic level papers. Alternatively, they can be longer and more complex in their structure, with opportunities for extended writing and the demonstration of the higher level skills of interpretation and evaluation. In this form they are very suitable for Higher level papers.

In a structured question, the question is divided into parts (a), (b), (c), etc. These parts can be further subdivided into (i), (ii), (iii), (iv), etc. A structure is built into the question and hence into your answer. This is where the term structured question comes from.

For each part of the question there are a number of lines or a space for your answer. This is a guide to you about the detail required in the answer, but it does not have to limit you. If you require more space continue your answer on a separate sheet of paper, but make sure you label the answer clearly, e.g. 3(a)(ii).

For each part of the question there is a number in brackets, e.g. (3), to show you how many marks are allocated to this part of the question by the examiner. If a part is worth three marks, for example, the question requires more than one or two words. As a general rule, if there are three marks allocated, you will need to make three points.

To give you a guide as you work through structured questions, papers are often designed to enable you to score one mark per minute. A question worth a maximum of fifteen marks should therefore take about fifteen minutes to answer.

You do not have to write your answers in full sentences. Concise notes are often the most suitable response. Read your answers to yourself, not aloud, and check that they make sense.

Like all questions, it is most important to read the stimulus material in the question thoroughly and more than once. This information is often not used fully by students and, as a result, the question is not answered fully. The key to answering many of these questions comes from the appreciation of the full meaning of the 'command word' at the start of the question – 'state', 'describe', 'explain'. The following glossary of command words may help you in the answering of structured questions.

- **State** This means a brief answer is required, with no supporting evidence. Alternatives include **write down**, **give**, **list**, **name**.
- **Define** Just a definition is required.
- **State and explain** A short answer is required (see **state**) but then an explanation is required. A question of this type should be worth more than one mark.
- **Describe** This is often used with reference to a particular experiment. The important points should be given about each stage. Again this type of question is worth more than one mark.
- **Outline** The answer should be brief and the main points picked out.
- **Predict** A brief answer is required, without supporting evidence. You are required to make logical links between various pieces of information.
- **Complete** You are required to add information to a diagram, sentence, flow chart, graph, key, table, etc.
- **Find** This is a general term which may mean calculate, measure, determine, etc.
- **Calculate** A numerical answer is required. You should show your working in order to get an answer. Do not forget the correct units.
- **Suggest** There is not just one correct answer, or you are applying your answer to a situation outside the syllabus.

Free response questions

These can include essay questions. In this type of question you are given a question which enables you to develop your answer in different ways. Your answer really is a free response and you write as much as you wish. Candidates often do not write enough or try to 'pad out' the answer. Remember you can only score marks when your answer matches the marking points on the examiner's marking scheme.

In this type of question it is important to plan your answer before starting it, allocating the correct amount of time to each part of the question.

DOUBLE SCIENCE AND SINGLE SCIENCE

Double Science is a good preparation for GCE A level courses as it requires you to study Physics, Chemistry and Biology to a standard sufficient to start an A level course. If you are preparing for Double Science you need to study all of the Units in this book.

If, however, you are only taking Single Science you need only study Units 1, 2, 5, 6, 9, 10 and 11.

ASSESSMENT OBJECTIVES IN SCIENCE

Assessment Objectives are the intellectual and practical skills you should be able to show. Opportunities must be made by the Examiner when setting the examination paper for you to demonstrate your mastery of these skills when you answer the question paper.

Traditionally, the Assessment Objective of knowledge and understanding has been regarded as the most important skill to develop. Candidates have been directed to learn large bodies of knowledge to recall in the examination. Whilst not wanting in any way to devalue the learning of facts, it should be remembered that on modern papers knowledge and understanding can only contribute about half of the marks available. The other half of the marks are acquired by mastery of the other Assessment Objectives. These are:

- To communicate scientific observations, ideas and arguments effectively.
- To select and use reference materials and translate data from one form to another.
- To interpret, evaluate and make informed judgements from relevant facts, observations and phenomena.
- To solve qualitative and quantitative problems.

1 Communicate scientific observations, ideas and arguments effectively

(weighting on papers approximately 5–10%)

In any examination, communication of information to the examiner is of primary importance. Questions are built into the paper to test your ability to communicate scientific information. Often these questions require extended answers.

In this type of question it is important to look at your answer objectively after you have written it to try to judge whether your answer is communicating information effectively.

2 Select and use reference materials and translate data from one form to another *(weighting on papers approximately 10–15%)*

In questions testing this Assessment Objective you are frequently asked to pick information from a chart or table and use it in another form, e.g. to draw a graph, a pie chart, bar chart, etc. You may be asked to complete a table using information from a graph.

It is important to transfer the skills you have acquired in Mathematics to your work in Science.

Skill acquired	Approx. grade in GCSE Maths
Read information from graphs or simple diagrams	F
Work out simple percentages	F
Construct and use pie charts	F
Use graphs	E
Plot graphs from data provided. The axes and scales are given to you	E
Be able to draw the best line through points on a graph	C
Select the most appropriate axes and scales for graph plotting	B

It is reasonable, therefore, to conclude that at Higher level you might be required to use a blank piece of graph paper and choose your own scales and axes. Then you would plot the points and draw a line of best fit through the points. If you are doing this, remember:

❶ To draw your graph as large as possible on the graph paper by choosing scales appropriately. Avoid choosing scales where, for example, 3 small squares are equivalent to 5°C. It would be better if 1 small square was equivalent to 1°C or 2°C. With this type of graph drawing, marks are usually awarded for the choice of scales and for labelled axes.

❷ To plot each point with a dot or small cross. Circle the dot or cross to make its position clear.

❸ Your line of best fit, whether it is a straight line or a curve, does not have to go through all the points. Some points may not be in the correct place, even if you plotted them correctly, because of inaccuracies in the experiment or experimental error.

On a Central tier paper a similar graph may have to be drawn, but it would be more appropriate for the examiner to give you a grid with axes and scales given. Then you would only have to plot the points and draw the line of best fit. It would probably be worth fewer marks than a graph on the Higher tier paper.

3 Interpret, evaluate and make informed judgements from relevant facts, observations and phenomena *(weighting on papers approximately 10–15%)*

Questions testing this Assessment Objective are often difficult for candidates. It is much easier to test this on a Higher tier paper than on a Basic tier paper.

The command word 'suggest' is very frequently used, as the information given, perhaps in a paragraph, table, diagram or any combination of these, is open to more than one interpretation.

Look carefully at all of the information given and look for possible alternative interpretations before writing your answer.

4 Solve qualitative and quantitative problems *(weighting on papers approximately 10–15%)*

There is no shortage of opportunities to ask questions testing this Assessment Objective on Science GCSE papers. Again opportunities are greater, especially for solving quantitative problems, on Higher tier papers.

Qualitative problems can include writing equations and the use of qualitative tests, for example, to distinguish sulphuric and hydrochloric acids.

Quantitative problems include the full range of calculations. Remember, when attempting to carry out a calculation, to:

❶ Recall the correct formula. There is usually a mark for being able to recall the formula. The formulae you are required to know are given on p.6.

Remember if you cannot recall the formula you will be unable to score marks on other parts of the question which require you to use the formula.

❷ Use all of the information given to you. If the question gives relative atomic masses, they should be used.

❸ Show all of your working, so credit can be given if you do not get the correct answer but get some way through the question.

❹ Take care when substituting in a mathematical formula to be consistent in your units.

❺ Give correct units to your answers if there are units. Remember ratios, including relative atomic masses and relative densities, do not have units.

Throughout this book you will see questions where the question is designed to test Assessment Objectives other than knowledge and understanding.

Formulae that you should know

For Basic tier papers:

pressure = force ÷ area $p = \frac{F}{A}$

speed = distance ÷ time taken $v = \frac{s}{t}$

In addition, for Central tier papers:

For an ideal gas, $\frac{\text{pressure}_1 \times \text{volume}_1}{\text{temperature}_1} = \frac{\text{pressure}_2 \times \text{volume}_2}{\text{temperature}_2}$ $\frac{p_1V_1}{T_1} = \frac{p_2V_2}{T_2}$

work done = force × distance moved in direction of force $W = Fs$

power = energy transformed or work done ÷ time $P = \frac{W}{t}$

electrical energy (in kWh) = power (in kW) × time (in h)

moment of a force = size of force × perpendicular distance from force to pivot

in a balanced system, the sum of clockwise moments about a point = the sum of anticlockwise moments about that point

energy = potential difference × current × time $E = VIt$

energy supplied to raise temperature = mass × specific heat capacity × change in temperature $E = mc\Delta T$

force = mass × acceleration $F = ma$

acceleration = change in velocity ÷ time taken $a = \frac{v}{t}$

wave speed = frequency × wavelength $v = f\lambda$

In addition, for Further tier papers:

charge = current × time $Q = It$

potential difference = current × resistance $V = IR$

electric power = potential difference × current $P = VI$

weight = mass × gravitational field strength $w = mg$

kinetic energy = $^1/_2$ × mass × $(\text{speed})^2$ $\text{ke} = {^1/_2}mv^2$

change in gravitational potential energy = mass × gravitational field strength × change in height $\text{gpe} = mg\Delta h$

momentum = mass × velocity $p = mv$

REVISION SUMMARY

Photosynthesis is the ultimate source of food. Green plants and some bacteria are the only organisms which make food. Other organisms eat plants or animals which have eaten plants.

Photosynthesis involves the use of carbon dioxide (from the atmosphere) and water (from the soil). In the presence of chlorophyll and energy (from sunlight), plants make carbohydrates.

$$\underset{\text{carbon dioxide}}{6CO_2} + \underset{\text{water}}{6H_2O} + \text{energy} \rightarrow \underset{\text{glucose (a carbohydrate)}}{C_6H_{12}O_6} + \underset{\text{oxygen}}{6O_2}$$

Respiration is a chemical oxidation process where energy is released from glucose. It occurs in all living cells.

$$C_6H_{12}O_6 + 6O_2 \rightarrow 6CO_2 + 6H_2O + \text{energy}$$

The energy is produced in the form of adenosine triphosphate (ATP), which acts as the energy currency of the living organism. Energy is released and made available to the cell when ATP loses one of its phosphate groups to become adenosine diphosphate (ADP).

Respiration involves the **exchange** of gases between cells and their environment. The exchange takes place between the lungs and the blood. It is made possible by **breathing**, which is a mechanical process that moves air in and out of the lungs during inspiration and expiration.

The lungs are damaged by the constant irritation of tobacco smoke. The delicate cell walls of the air sacs (alveoli) are damaged. Smoking reduces the resistance to bacteria and viruses. It also reduces the efficiency of gas exchange. Tar causes **lung cancer**. Smoking tobacco during pregnancy reduces the amount of oxygen available to the developing foetus. Infection of the bronchial tubes can cause **bronchitis**.

Respiration can also take place in the absence of air or oxygen. This is called **anaerobic respiration**. Examples of anaerobic respiration include:

1. The action of yeast on glucose solution to produce ethanol and carbon dioxide. This is usually called fermentation.

$$C_6H_{12}O_6 \rightarrow 2C_2H_5OH + 2CO_2 + \text{energy}$$
$$\text{glucose} \rightarrow \text{ethanol} + \text{carbon dioxide}$$

2. In our muscles when oxygen is used up more quickly than it can be provided, e.g. during a race.

$$C_6H_{12}O_6 \rightarrow 2C_3H_6O_3 + \text{energy}$$
$$\text{glucose} \rightarrow \text{lactic acid}$$

Lactic acid is slightly poisonous and causes the muscles to ache and cramp. When oxygen is available the lactic acid is used up and the pain goes.

Various wastes produced from metabolism are removed by the kidneys, skin and lungs. The kidneys filter practically all the nitrogenous wastes from the blood. The skin removes water, salts and some urea in sweat. Sweat also helps to control body temperature.

Growth is the irreversible increase in the size of an organism involving the synthesis of protoplasm. It begins at the moment of fertilization, continues during gestation and goes on until the end of puberty.

Producing new offspring is called **reproduction**. There are two ways in which reproduction can occur – **sexual reproduction** and **asexual reproduction**. Sexual reproduction involves sex cells called **gametes**. These are produced by a form of cell division called **meiosis**. The diagram summarizes the changes which occur in the nuclei of cells during meiosis.

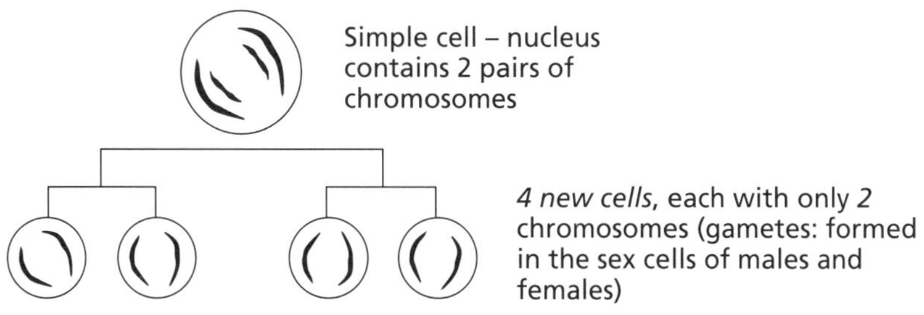

REVISION SUMMARY

The female gametes are called **egg cells** and the male gametes are called **sperm** in animals or **pollen** in plants. During the process of **fertilization** a male sex cell and a female sex cell fuse together to form a **zygote**. This develops by repeated cell division to produce an **embryo**. The zygote contains genetic information from *both* parents, so the offspring will not be identical to either the mother or the father.

Asexual reproduction requires only one parent and involves only a form of cell division called **mitosis**. The changes which occur in the nuclei of cells during mitosis are summarized in the diagram.

If you need to revise this subject more thoroughly, see the relevant topics in the *Letts GCSE Science Study Guide.*

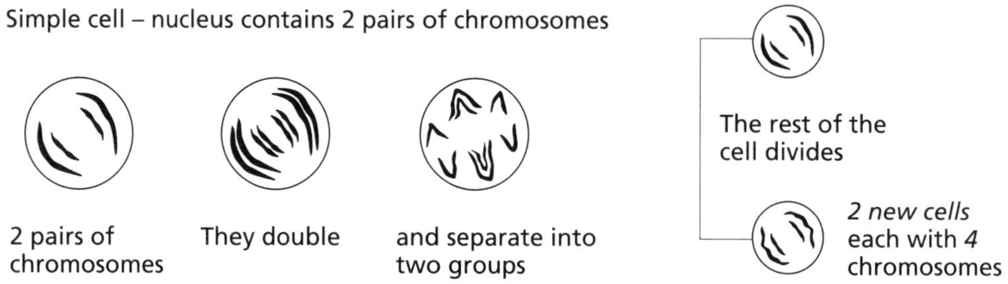

Each new cell is an exact copy of the original. A geranium plant can be used to produce new geraniums by taking stem cuttings. Underground storage organs (e.g. potatoes) and plants sending out runners (e.g. strawberries) are forms of vegetative propagation.

There are six important **senses**: namely sight, hearing, taste, touch, smell and temperature. Changes which are detected by **receptors** in the sensory organs are called **stimuli**. These stimuli bring about changes in our bodies in two different ways.

❶ Messages (called **impulses**) can be sent through the **Central Nervous System** (CNS), which is composed of the brain and spinal cord. They communicate with all parts of the body via nerves. These impulses can lead to two types of action – **reflex actions** and **conscious actions**. Reflex actions, such as removing a hand from a hot surface, occur very quickly to avoid damage and the impulses are sent by the most direct route through **reflex arcs**. Impulses for conscious actions take a longer route via the brain and occur more slowly.

❷ A much slower method of sending messages around the body uses chemical messengers called **hormones**. The hormone system consists of a number of glands which release hormones into the bloodstream. The hormones are then carried around the body until they reach the appropriate organ. Examples include:

Hormone	Produced in	Effect of the hormone
Growth hormone	Pituitary gland	Speeds up growth
Insulin	Pancreas	Controls the amount of sugar in blood
Female sex hormone	Ovaries	Controls menstrual cycle and sexual development

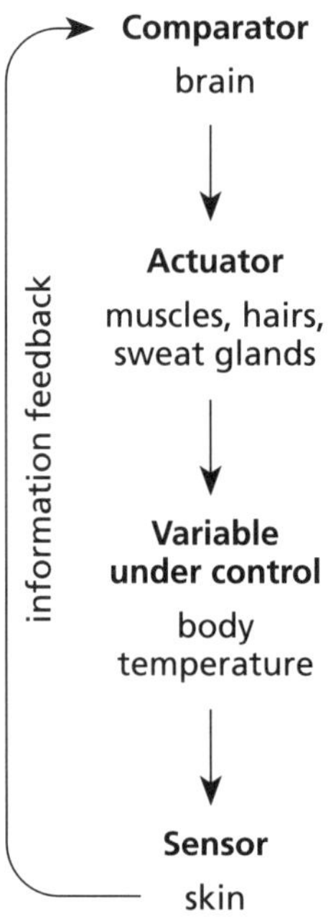

The CNS can be affected by alcohol, tobacco and drugs. Four types of drug which can affect the brain and CNS are **sedatives**, e.g. alcohol and barbiturates (slow down thinking process and cause drowsiness), **stimulants**, e.g. cocaine, nicotine in tobacco and caffeine (speed up the brain and cause alertness), drugs which cause **hallucinations**, e.g. marijuana and LSD, and **painkillers**, e.g. paracetamol (remove the sense of pain).

Maintaining a constant condition in the body is called **homeostasis**. A change in constant condition is detected by the **sensor**. An output is sent by the controlling organ (called the **comparator**) to the **actuator** which makes the necessary change. The control of body temperature is summarized in the diagram in the margin.

Other homeostatic systems include control of the amount of glucose in the body and control of the amount of light entering the eye.

QUESTIONS

1

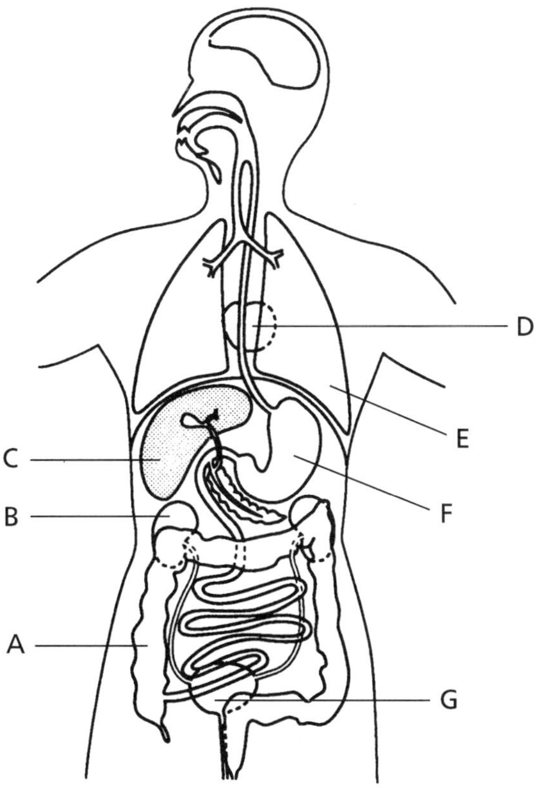

The diagram shows some of the organs in a human body.
For **each** of the organs labelled, write down its name and write a sentence to describe its job. (14)

A ....

....

B ....

....

C ....

....

D ....

....

E ....

....

QUESTIONS

F ....

....

G ....

....

2 Leaves are organs of photosynthesis. They come in all shapes and sizes but all of them are adapted to absorb as much light as possible.

(a) Give **one** way in which leaves are adapted to absorb light.

.... (1)

(b) The diagram shows a cross-section through a leaf.

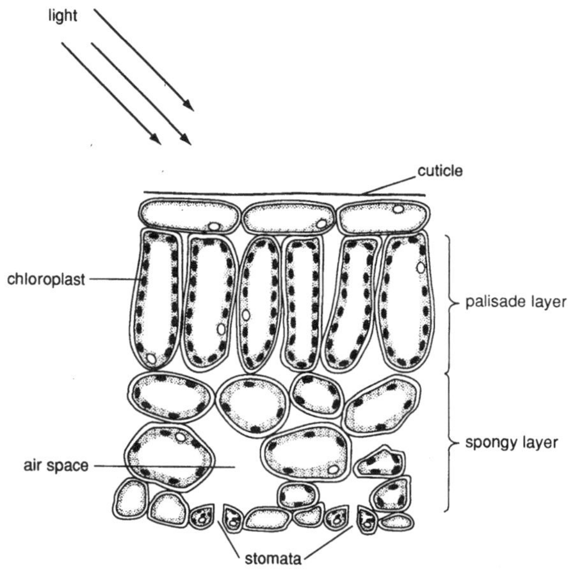

Explain the following observations:

(i) The cuticle is transparent.

.... (1)

(ii) Most chloroplasts are found in the palisade layer.

.... (1)

(iii) Air spaces are found mostly in the spongy layer.

.... (1)

(c) What is the substance in chloroplasts which absorbs light?

.... (1)

(d) Explain how each of the following affects the rate of photosynthesis in a potted plant.

(i) Moving it nearer to the window.

.... (1)

(ii) Moving it to a colder room.

.... (1)

(e) Complete the word equation for photosynthesis.

.... + water → carbohydrates + ... (1)

MEG 1994

3 (a) (i) The diagram shows part of the human female reproductive system.

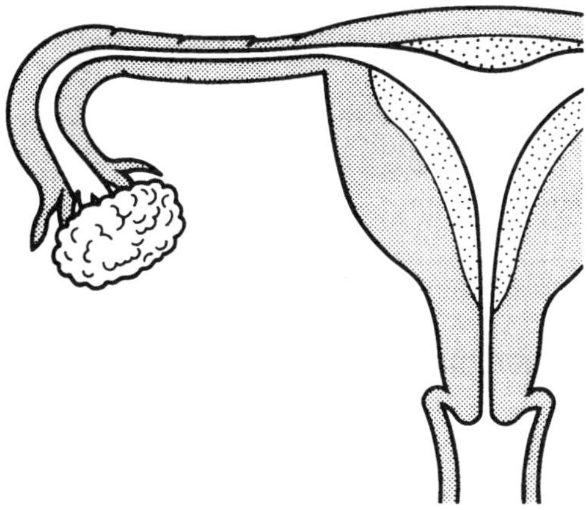

Use an **S** to mark on the diagram the place where the sperm are released during intercourse and an **F** to show where fertilization usually occurs. (2)

(ii) Explain how the structure of a sperm enables it to travel from **S** to **F**.

....

.... (2)

(b) A few weeks after fertilization, the fertilized egg becomes an embryo which is surrounded by amniotic fluid.

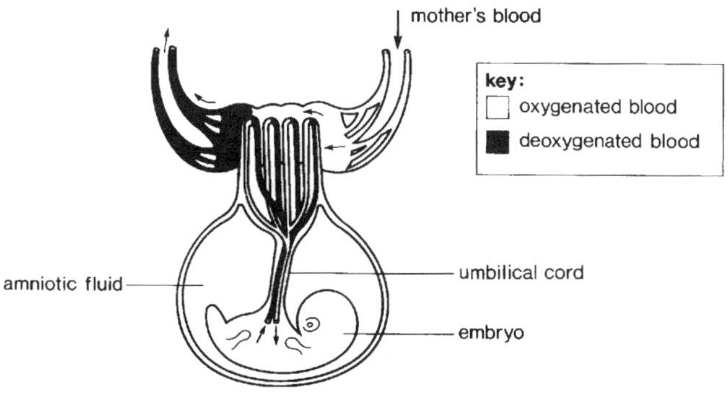

QUESTIONS

(i) Describe **two** functions of the amniotic fluid.

....

....

.... (2)

(ii) Describe how the oxygen level in the blood of the embryo is maintained.

....

....

....

.... (3)

MEG 1994

4 The regulation of body temperature is achieved by balancing energy release against energy loss. Energy release is greater during exercise.

(a) The rate of metabolism changes during exercise. Describe how this influences energy release.

....

....

.... (2)

(b) Explain why, during exercise, the body attempts to lose more energy.

....

....

.... (2)

(c) During rest, excess blood sugar is stored. How is this achieved?

....

....

.... (2)

(d) The graphs show how the blood glucose level and the concentration of hormone involved in glucose storage vary over a 12-hour time period.

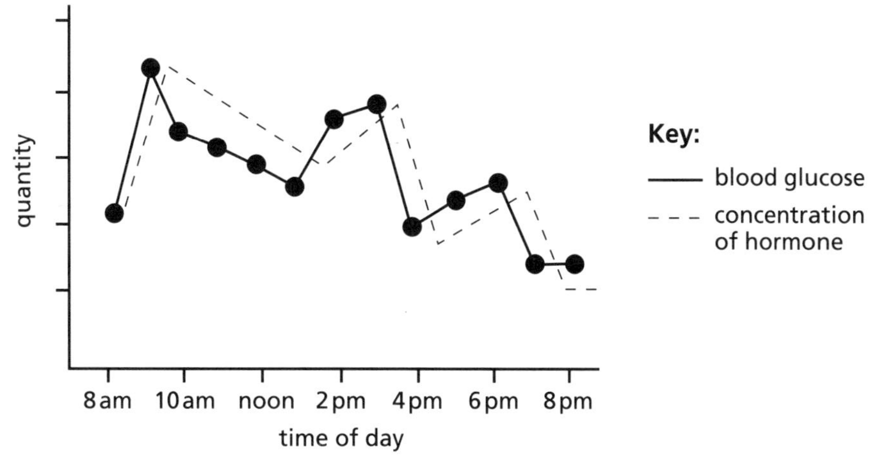

(i) Using these graphs explain why a single daily dose of hormone would not adequately control blood glucose concentration in diabetics.

....

....

.... (2)

(ii) Explain how physical exercise would influence the production of the hormone involved in glucose storage.

....

....

.... (2)

MEG 1994

2 Inheritance and evolution

REVISION SUMMARY

We inherit characteristics from our parents. The study of the way in which we inherit these characteristics is called **genetics**. Information is passed on by **genes**. A **gene** is a section of **DNA (deoxyribonucleic acid) polymer**. A number of these genes make up the **chromosomes** which are found in the **nucleus** of a **cell**. In a human, all cells (apart from sex cells) contain 46 chromosomes arranged in 23 **homologous pairs**.

There are two ways in which cell division can occur – **mitosis** and **meiosis**. In mitosis exact copies of cells are produced. The original chromosomes make copies of themselves and the cell divides to produce two new cells which contain the same chromosomes as the original cell. This process occurs when an organism grows and when an organism reproduces asexually, forming **clones**.

Sex cells (eggs and sperm) are produced by meiosis. These cells contain half the number of chromosomes of a normal cell. In a human there are 23 chromosomes in each sex cell. In **fertilization** 23 chromosomes from the mother combine with 23 chromosomes from the father. The offspring contains 46 chromosomes (23 pairs), with half coming from the mother and half from the father.

The sex of a baby is determined by a pair of sex chromosomes. There are two types of sex chromosome.

❶ The long **X** chromosome. ❷ The short **Y** chromosome.

The cells in a female contain two **X** chromosomes (**XX**) and in a male the cells contain one **X** and one **Y** chromosome (**XY**). The diagram shows how males and females are produced.

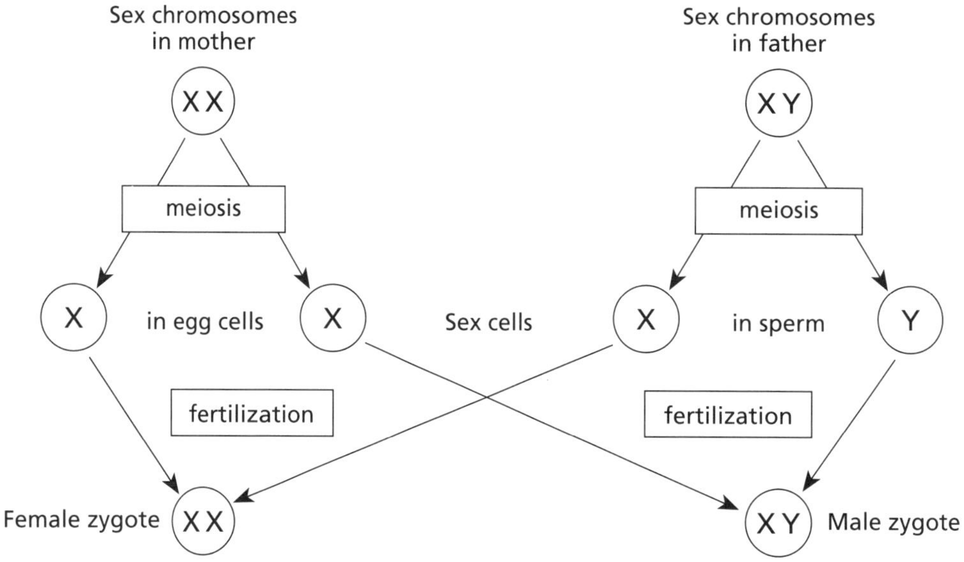

Often a particular characteristic is determined by a pair of genes. One gene in the pair has come from the mother and one from the father. One of the genes may be **dominant** and the other **recessive**. If a dominant gene is present, it will decide the characteristic.

Eye colour is determined by genes. Genes which control the same characteristic are called **alleles**. Two alleles can be **B** (the dominant allele which produces brown eyes) and **b** (the recessive allele which produces blue eyes). There are three possible combinations of alleles (called **genotypes**) **BB**, **Bb** (or **bB**) and **bb**. A child who inherits the genotypes **BB** or **Bb** will have brown eyes because the presence of the dominant **B** allele and a child who inherits the genotype **bb** will have blue eyes.

Genotypes which contain two identical alleles (e.g. **BB** or **bb**) are said to be **homozygous**. Genotypes which contain two different alleles are called **heterozygous**. The diagrams on the next page, called Punnett squares, summarize what happens when parents with different eye colour have children.

	BB (brown eyes)	
bb (blue eyes)	Bb	Bb
	Bb	Bb

all brown eyes

	Bb (brown eyes)	
bb (blue eyes)	Bb	bb
	Bb	bb

50% blue eyes/50% brown eyes

Different genes control other characteristics in the same way. In some cases, however, the gene which controls a characteristic is not present in the shorter **Y** chromosome. In the male there is only one gene present (on the **X** chromosome) and this alone determines the characteristic. Some conditions, such as colour blindness and haemophilia, are sex-linked and occur predominantly in males because the gene is recessive on the **X** chromosome. Other conditions, such as cystic fibrosis, are produced by a recessive gene which can show equally in males and females.

Selective breeding is used by scientists to improve the desirable characteristics in plants and animals. This requires identification of the characteristic which needs to be improved, e.g. yield, fat-to-lean ratio in a meat carcase. Parents are chosen which show the characteristic required and breeding takes place. Offspring are chosen which show the characteristic required and the process is repeated.

Genetic engineering involves the replacement of one gene from a chromosome with another gene from another organism which has improved characteristics. In an attempt to produce a true blue rose, scientists are replacing the gene which causes colour in the rose by the gene which makes petunia flowers blue. This process has also been used to produce antibiotics and hormones.

Variation within a species occurs in various ways. A sudden change in a species can occur by a **mutation** in the genetic information. Some mutations can be beneficial, while others are harmful.

Charles Darwin (1809–1882) studied the **theory of evolution** and suggested how, over millions of years, simple creatures could have developed (evolved) into new organisms by a process of **evolution**. This occurred by **natural selection**. Three important principles of natural selection are:

1. variations within a species,
2. survival of the fittest,
3. adaptation of organisms.

Chromosomes are made up from DNA, which is a complex polymer made up from four different monomers called **nucleotides**. These nucleotides consist of an organic base molecule, a sugar molecule and a phosphate group linked together. DNA consists of a double helix. The sides of the ladder are composed of alternate sugar (S) and phosphate (P) groups. The rungs of the ladder consist of pairs of organic bases which are weakly bonded together by hydrogen bonds. There are four bases – adenine (A), thymine (T), cytosine (C) and guanine (G). These bases always pair across the double helix in the same way.

A with T and C with G

All living things contain protein, and protein synthesis is a key process in the living organism. The bases inside the gene are a code for the production of a specific protein. DNA is contained in the nucleus of the cell, but protein synthesis takes place in the cytoplasm. A messenger molecule (RNA) carries this code into the cytoplasm. In the cytoplasm the RNA acts as a template for the building of proteins.

When DNA makes a copy of itself (**replication**) the two halves of the double helix unwind and separate from one end. As the unwinding occurs, nucleotides form new bonds and two new double helices start to form.

If you need to revise this subject more thoroughly, see the relevant topics in the *Letts GCSE Science Study Guide.*

QUESTIONS

1 The features of humans are either inherited or are caused by environmental influences.

accidental loss of an arm
blood group
eye colour
gender/sex
mass

(a) From the features listed choose:

(i) one which is controlled by environmental influences only,

.... (1)

(ii) one which is controlled by inheritance only,

.... (1)

(iii) one which is controlled by both environmental influences and inheritance.

.... (1)

(b) Which part of the cell nucleus enables features to be passed on from one generation to the next?

.... (1)

MEG 1994

2 (a) Complete the diagram below to show how the sex of a child depends on the chromosomes the child inherits.

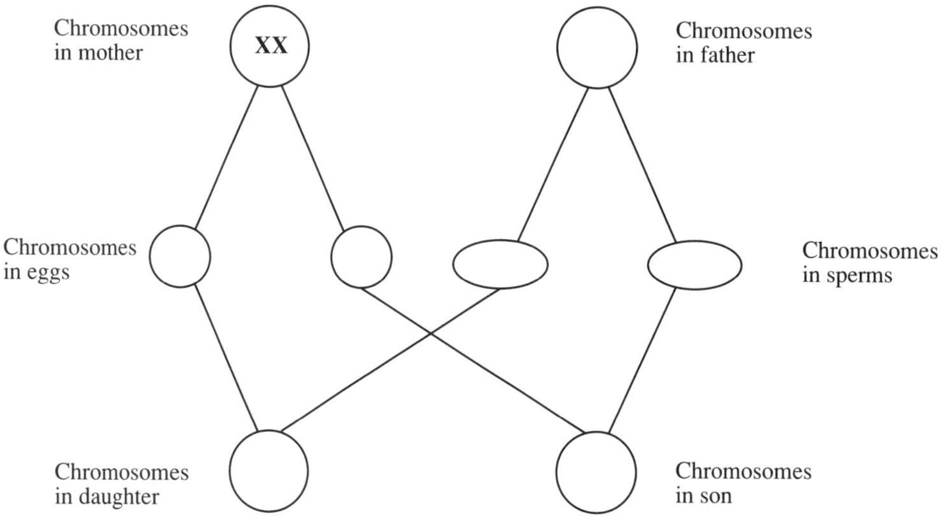

(3)

QUESTIONS

(b) The diagram below shows the inheritance of Huntington's chorea in a family.

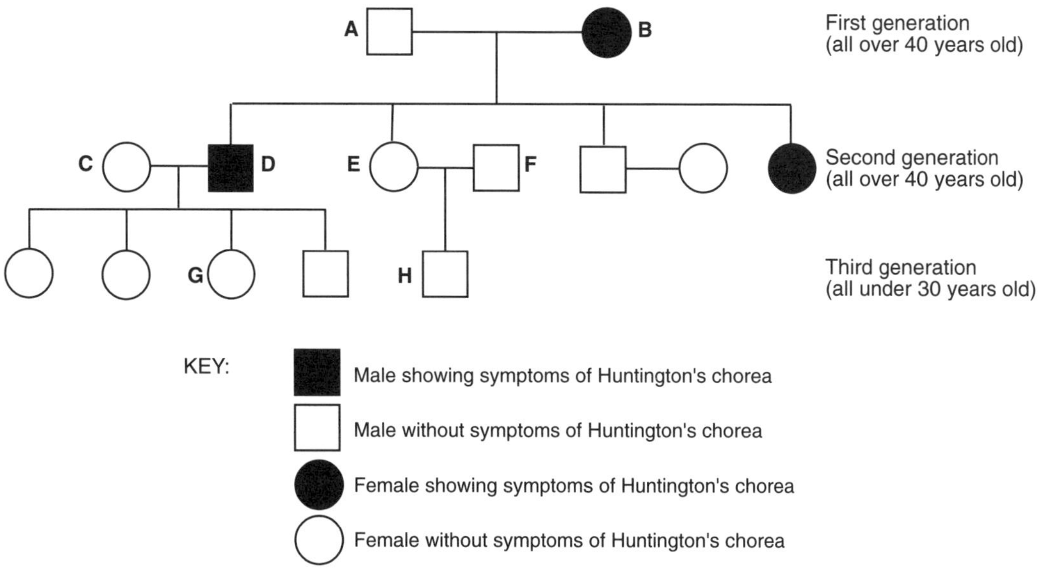

Symptoms of Huntington's chorea usually develop between the ages of 35 and 40.

What is the chance that the following will develop Huntington's chorea?

G ....

H ....

Explain the reasons for your answers as fully as you can. You may use genetic diagrams if you wish.

....

....

....

....

....

....

.... (6)

NEAB 1995

QUESTIONS

3 The table shows how the average milk yield per Ayrshire cow increased between 1807 and 1967.

Year	Average yield of milk per cow (litres per year)
1807	1934
1855	2570
1955	3567
1967	4004

(a) Explain, as fully as you can, how farmers might have increased the amount of milk yielded by cows.

....

....

....

.... (3)

(b) Give **two** advantages in having cows which produce higher yields of milk.

....

.... (2)

NEAB 1994

4 Cells that produce eggs and sperm divide by a process called meiosis. Other body cells divide by mitosis. The diagram shows a cell with four chromosomes.

Explain, using diagrams to aid your answer, how this cell can divide by mitosis. (4)

QUESTIONS

5 The peppered moth has light-coloured wings 'peppered' with dark spots and bars. In 1850 a dark variety of this moth, with almost black wings, was discovered in Manchester. After 1850, the dark form rapidly became more and more common, so that today, in the Manchester area, the light-coloured variety is rare. The light-coloured variety still continues to thrive in some other parts of the United Kingdom.

(a) Suggest how the original dark-coloured variety came into existence.

....

....

.... (2)

(b) Explain why the dark-coloured variety has now become the common variety in the Manchester area.

....

.... (2)

SEG 1994

6 (a) The diagram shows a portion of a DNA molecule during replication. The letters A, C, G and T represent the four bases: A = adenine; C = cytosine; G = guanine; T = thymine.

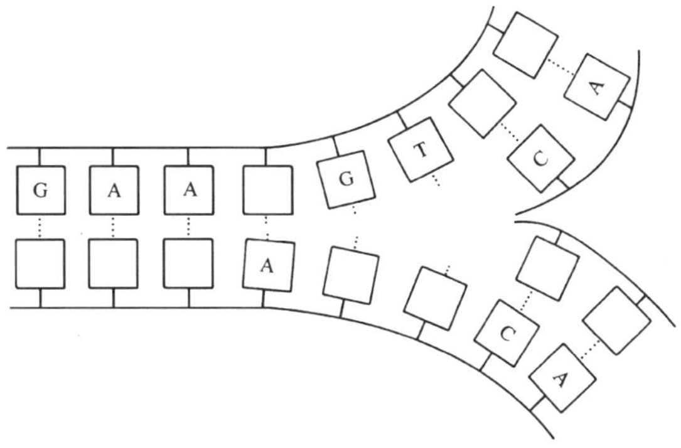

Complete the diagram by writing in the correct letters (A, C, G or T) in the empty boxes. (2)

(b) In mitosis, why is it necessary for exact copies of the DNA to be passed to each new cell?

....

....

.... (2)

QUESTIONS

(c) The order of the bases in a DNA molecule acts as a code that enables a cell to make proteins.
The table shows the codes for some of the amino acids found in human cells.

Amino Acid	DNA code	Amino acid	DNA code
Phenylalanine	AAA	Leucine	AAT
Tyrosine	ATA	Cysteine	ACA
Histidine	GTA	Glutamine	GTT
Isoleucine	TAA	Methionine	TAC
Asparagine	TTA	Lysine	TTT
Valine	GAA	Alanine	CGA
Glutamic acid	CTT	Glycine	CCA

(i) Complete the box to show the amino acids which would be linked if the code of bases was:

DNA sequence TAACCAACA

Amino acid sequence

(1)

(ii) In the box below, write down the sequence of bases which would act as a code for the following chain of amino acids:

Amino acids Alanine, Valine, Histidine

DNA sequence

(1)

(d) Changes in base sequence can occur when a DNA molecule replicates. These changes may lead to altered genes.

(i) What name is given to the changes in DNA which can cause altered genes?

.... (1)

(ii) Name **one** human disease which is caused by a faulty gene.

.... (1)

(iii) Explain why changes made during the replication of DNA can sometimes benefit a species of animal or plant.

....

.... (2)

ULEAC 1994

Letts Q&A

Populations and human influences

REVISION SUMMARY

The population of living organisms can increase very rapidly. The sketch graph shows the usual exponential increase of a typical population of organisms, e.g. animals, plants, bacteria, etc.

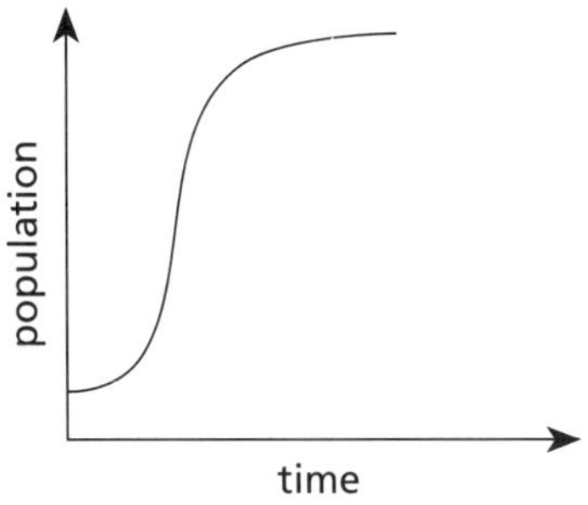

The growth of a population slows down due to

- competition for food and living space;
- build up of toxic wastes;
- introduction of **predators**.

Birth rate and death rate are expressed as yearly percentages, and are used to calculate population growth. A birth rate of 15% means that for every 100 individuals at the beginning of the year, there are 15 more at the end of the year (i.e. 115). A death rate of 5% means that for every 100 individuals at the beginning of the year, there would be 5 less at the end of the year (i.e. 95). This population would show an increase of $15 - 5 = 10\%$.

The increase of the human population has lead to an increase in the exploitation of raw materials. Industry and farming has lead to an increase in the use of raw materials. Industry and farming produce goods and food on a massive scale. This has benefits for the population in the form of jobs leading to prosperity and a higher standard of living. However, there is a detrimental effect on the environment. There are increasing problems concerning the

- disposal of our waste;
- pollution of rivers, lakes and seas;
- extensive use of fertilizers causing **eutrophication** of water systems;
- reduction of tropical rain forests.

This increase in development has caused a change in the **biosphere**. The biosphere is that part of the Earth and its atmosphere which is inhabited by living things.

The increase in carbon dioxide in the air has led to the **greenhouse effect**, which causes global warming.

CFCs (chlorofluorocarbons) are released into the atmosphere causing holes to be formed in the **ozone layer** in the upper atmosphere. The ozone layer protects us on the Earth from the harmful ultraviolet rays which can cause skin cancer.

Acid rain is due to the increase in sulphur dioxide and nitrogen oxides being emitted into the atmosphere from the burning of fossil fuels. These gases react with water in the atmosphere to produce sulphuric and nitric acids. The acids will then react with metals and some rocks (e.g. limestone) and reduce the pH of water in rivers and lakes.

If you need to revise this subject more thoroughly, see the relevant topics in the *Letts GCSE Science Study Guide.*

QUESTIONS

1 In 1950, near Long Island, USA, a group of scientists studied the breeding colonies of the osprey. Ospreys are birds that only eat live fish. The food chain shows a source of the ospreys' food.

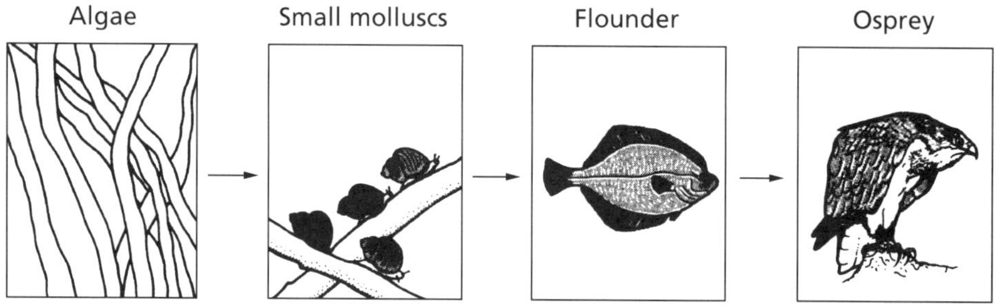

(a) From this food chain, write down an example of:

(i) a producer;

.... (1)

(ii) a primary consumer.

.... (1)

(iii) It is possible to construct a pyramid of numbers for this food chain. How would the number of molluscs compare with the number of ospreys?

....

.... (1)

(b)

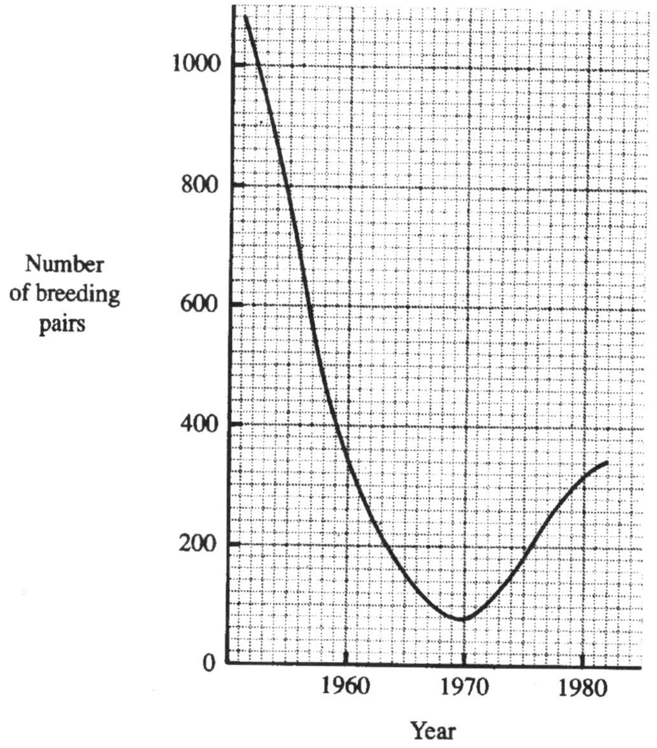

QUESTIONS

The graph shows how the number of breeding pairs of osprey in a colony near Long Island changed between 1950 and 1980.

(i) By 1965 local people believed the sea near Long Island was polluted. Using the previous information, what evidence was there to suggest that the sea was polluted?

....

.... (1)

(ii) It was found that part of the 'pollution' of the sea was caused by a pesticide called DDT. This was being used to kill mosquitoes which lived in the area. From the graph, find when the use of DDT was stopped.

.... (1)

(iii) It was found that the concentration of DDT in an osprey was much greater than that in the algae. Explain why.

....

.... (1)

SEG 1994

2 Two groups of pupils carried out surveys in eight different parts of their local river, (shown as A–H on the map). The surveys were carried out in early summer.

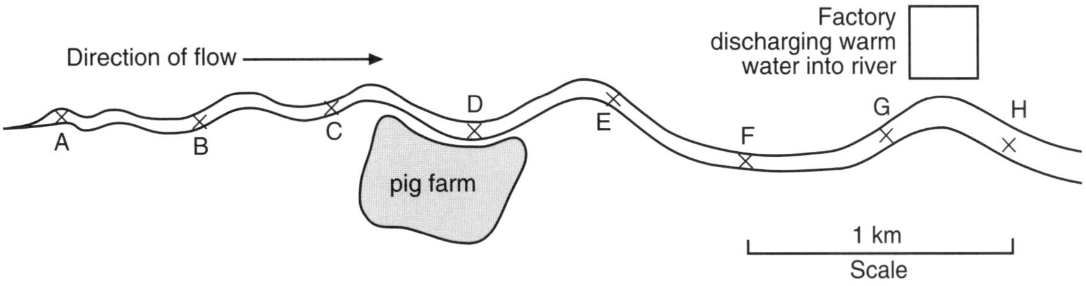

(a) One group was comparing the concentration of oxygen in the water with the number of mayfly nymphs. Their results are shown on the graph.

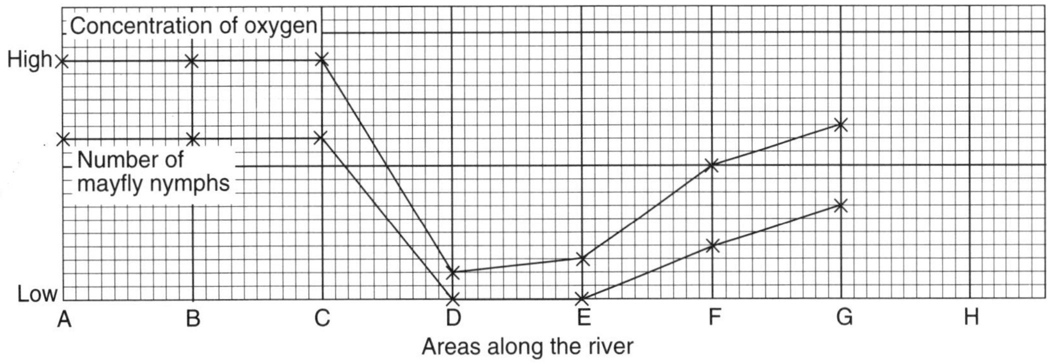

Letts Q&A

QUESTIONS

(i) Describe what happens to the concentration of oxygen in the water as it flows from **C** to **G**.

....

.... (1)

(ii) A leak of liquid waste from the pig farm could cause this sudden change in the concentration of oxygen. Explain how.

....

.... (2)

(iii) Explain how this change in oxygen concentration will affect the fish.

....

.... (2)

(iv) An area of water in another river contains lots of mayfly nymphs. What should the pupils be able to say about the concentration of oxygen in the water?

....

.... (1)

(b) The other group investigated the feeding relationships at areas **A**, **B** and **C**. The food web below shows some of their results.

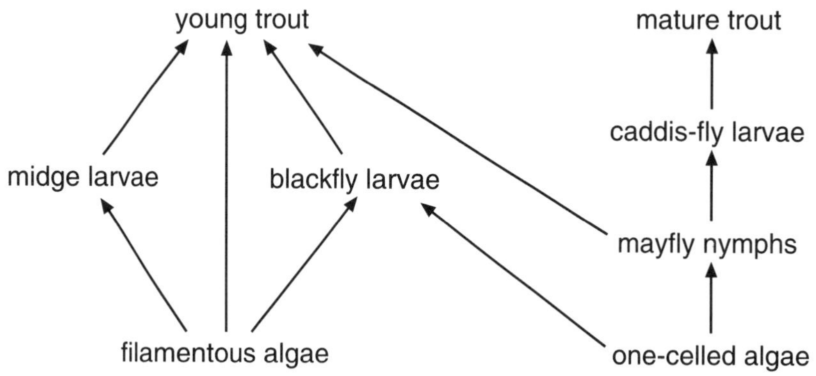

(i) The pupils knew that the blackfly larvae change into flies and fly away.

[A] This change could cause the population of mayfly nymphs to go **down**. Explain why.

....

.... (2)

[B] This change could cause the population of mayfly nymphs to go **up**.
Explain why.

....

.... (2)

(ii) The pupils used their knowledge about the number of links in a food chain to conclude that young trout got more of the Sun's energy than did the mature trout. Explain how they came to this conclusion.

....

....

....

.... (4)

(c) One of the pupils read that 'oxygen is less soluble in warm water than it is in cold water.' Use this fact to predict the likely population of trout at area **H**, compared to the population at area **C**. Give an explanation for your prediction.

Prediction: At **H** the number of trout will ....

Explanation: ....

....

....

.... (4)

SEG 1995

4 Ecology

REVISION SUMMARY

Only a small amount of the Sun's energy that falls onto a plant is transferred into the plant's tissues and food stores. When a rabbit eats the plant only about one-tenth of the energy in the plant is transferred to the body of the rabbit. The rest of the energy is lost as the rabbit moves, respires, through excretion and body heat. The same principle applies when a rabbit is eaten by a fox.

Energy flow in a food chain can be expressed in a pyramid of numbers and a pyramid of biomass. As there is a loss of energy at each level of the food chain, the number of organisms that can be supported at each level becomes less. This drop in numbers at each level of a food chain is expressed as a **pyramid of numbers**. This drop in numbers of organisms can also be expressed as a reduction in the total mass of living material at each level. This is called the **pyramid of biomass**.

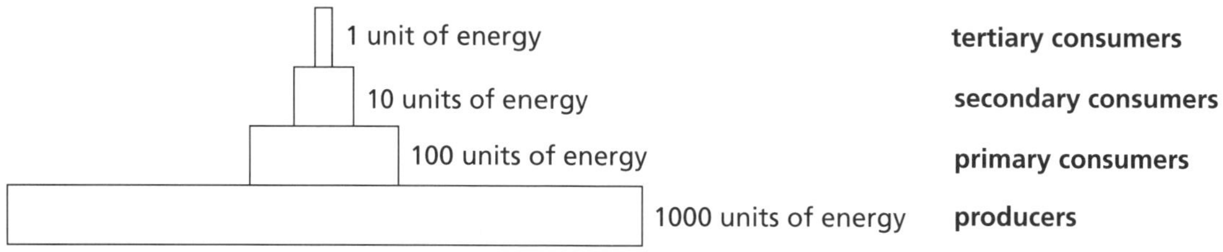

not to scale

Carbon and nitrogen are important elements that are **recycled** naturally. Within the **carbon cycle** photosynthesis is the only process that removes carbon dioxide from the atmosphere. Carbon dioxide is returned to the atmosphere during the processes of **combustion**, **respiration** and **decay**.

Plants cannot use the element nitrogen from the atmosphere; nitrogen-fixing bacteria convert nitrogen in the air into useful nitrogen compounds in the soil. Plants absorb nitrates and turn them into amino acids, which are used to build up proteins. Nitrogen is also returned to the soil by lightning, decaying plants and animals and excretion.

Decay enables chemicals to be **recycled**. There are three main groups of **decomposers** – **bacteria**, **fungi** and **soil invertebrates**. The conditions necessary for decay are **warmth**, **moisture** and **oxygen**. Decay is an important process in the treatment of sewage and the formation of compost.

With the need for more food, **intensive farming** methods were introduced. Small fields were combined to form large fields. Large machinery then made farming more efficient. Removal of hedges removed the habitat of some plants and animals and soil erosion increased.

Ecosystems need to be correctly managed to prevent environmental damage. Intensive farming methods and overgrazing can cause soil erosion. Tropical rainforests are an example of an ecosystem managed incorrectly. The deforestation has ruined the soil, encouraged flooding and soil erosion, and caused changes to the local climate. It has also killed wildlife on a massive scale and increased the concentration of carbon dioxide in the atmosphere, contributing to the greenhouse effect.

It has become necessary to conserve ecosystems to prevent the loss of unique areas, such as wetlands and rainforests, thus hopefully preventing the extinction of endangered species. The Government has enforced conservation of marine stocks by introducing fishing quotas and regulations on the mesh sizes of nets. This hopefully ensures we do not remove fish faster than they can be replaced by the natural process of reproduction.

If you need to revise this subject more thoroughly, see the relevant topics in the Letts GCSE *Science Study Guide*.

Letts Q&A

1 Gardeners put leaves and weeds in a compost heap.

They leave this to rot into a peaty compost which is rich in plant nutrients, and can be used to improve soil fertility.

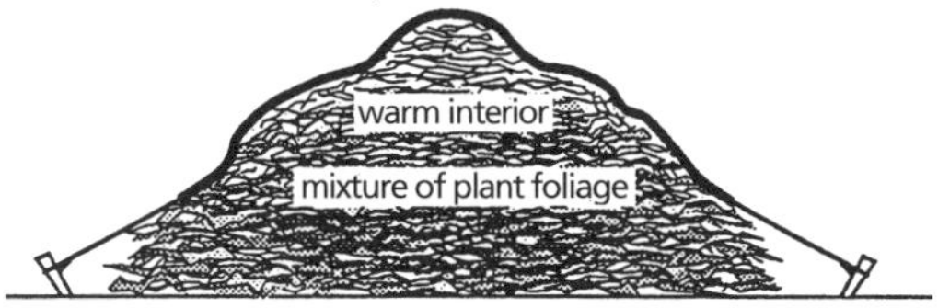

Three gardeners living in different parts of Britain made compost heaps on the same day in spring.

To speed up the rotting process they covered them with plastic sheets and mixed them up each week using a fork.

The table gives some information about where the gardeners lived.

Gardener	Town	Average temperature/°C	Average annual rainfall/cm
A	London	13.2	61.0
B	Manchester	12.0	85.9
C	Edinburgh	11.0	69.9

(a) (i) Suggest which gardener's compost heap will be ready first.

.... (1)

(ii) Explain your answer.

.... (1)

(b) How does mixing up the heap help speed up rotting?

....

.... (1)

(c) The gardener in Manchester forgot to replace the plastic sheet over his compost heap. Explain how this might affect the rotting.

....

.... (1)

MEG 1994

2 A community in a woodland consists of oak trees, caterpillars, voles and owls.
Many thousands of caterpillars feed on the leaves of a single oak tree.
A single vole may eat a hundred caterpillars each day.
An owl may eat three voles in one day.

(a) The diagram shows four pyramids of numbers.

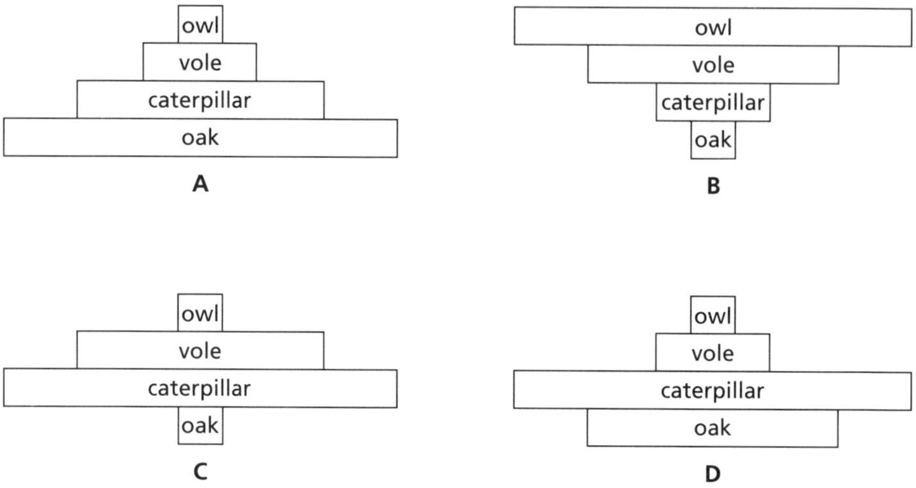

(i) Which pyramid of numbers is correct for this woodland community?

.... (1)

(ii) What is meant by the term biomass?

.... (1)

(iii) Draw a pyramid of biomass for the woodland community. (2)

(iv) Explain how energy is lost to the surroundings between each level of your pyramid of biomass.

....

.... (1)

(b) In a town near to the woodland many additional houses and factories are built. Suggest and explain **one** effect this might have on the woodland community.

Effect: ....

....

Explanation: ....

.... (2)

MEG 1994

3 The diagram shows energy flow through a rabbit in one year.

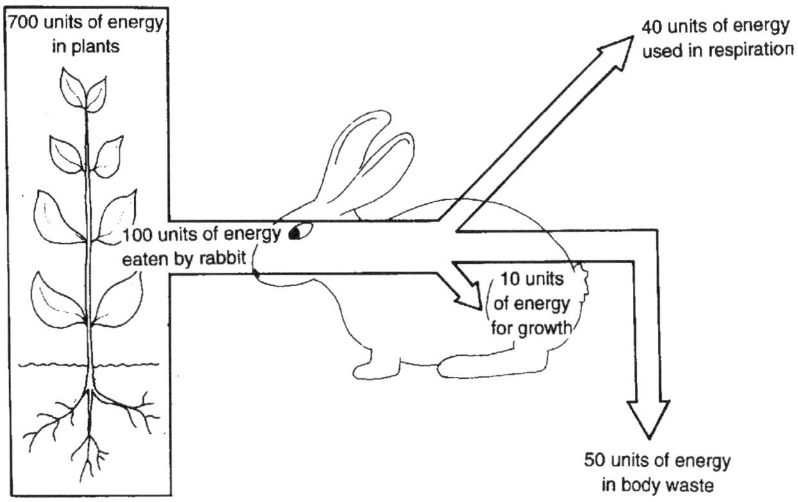

(a) From what source do plants obtain their energy?

.... (1)

(b) For every 700 units of energy in the plants, only 100 units are transferred to the rabbit. Write down **two** reasons why the rabbit does not get **all** the energy from the plants.

1 ....

....

2 ....

.... (2)

(c) For every 100 units of energy eaten by the rabbit 50 units of energy are transferred as body waste. One example is the removal of undigested food in faeces.

(i) Write down the name of another process that contributes to the 50 units lost as body waste.

.... (1)

QUESTIONS

(ii) How many units of the 50 are likely to be lost in faeces?

Choose from 5, 10, 20 or 40 units. .... (1)

(d) Stoats are predators on rabbits. Four possible pyramids of biomass are drawn below.

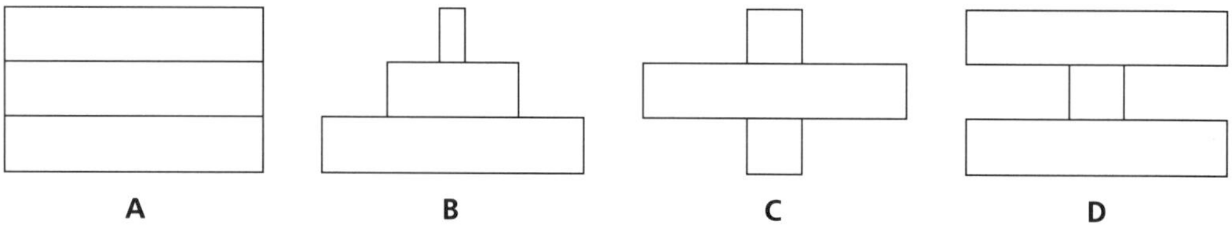

(i) Which **one** of the four pyramids correctly shows the relationship between plants, rabbits and stoats?

.... (1)

(ii) What **two** measurements are used to estimate the biomass of a population of rabbits?

1 ....

2 .... (2)

(e) Rabbits can be a major pest by feeding on farmers' crops. One farmer tries to control the number of rabbits by regularly shooting them. Another farmer tries to encourage natural predators, such as stoats and hawks, by leaving rough corners of fields to act as wildlife habitats.

Complete the table to show **one** advantage and **one** disadvantage of each control method.

	Rabbits controlled by regular shooting	Rabbits controlled by natural predators
Advantage		
Disadvantage		

(4)

MEG 1994

Substances can be separated or purified by a series of techniques. A mixture of insoluble and soluble materials, such as salt and sand, can be separated by dissolving one of the substances in a suitable solvent, water in the case of salt and sand, and **filtering**. The insoluble residue, sand, remains on the filter paper. The salt can be recovered from the solution by **evaporation**.

Distillation can be used to separate a liquid from a solid. Distillation consists of boiling followed by condensation. Mixtures of substances with boiling points close together, e.g. a mixture of liquids, can be separated by **fractional distillation**.

Chromatography is used to separate mixtures of substances in solution, e.g. a mixture of dyes.

A pure substance has a sharp melting point. An impure substance contains impurities and melts at a lower temperature than the pure substance and over a range of temperature.

The chemical elements (see Unit 6) are arranged in order of increasing atomic number in the Periodic Table. Elements with similar properties are in the same vertical column (or **group**). The horizontal rows are called **periods**. Common chemical families include: alkali metals – group I, alkaline earth metals – group II, halogens – group VII.

Atoms of the different elements are made up of different numbers of **protons**, **neutrons** and **electrons**. An atom always contains an equal number of protons and electrons. If an atom loses one or more electrons it forms a positive ion or **cation**. If an atom gains one or more electrons it forms a negative ion or **anion**. Atoms of the same element must contain the same number of protons and electrons, but can contain different numbers of neutrons. These are called **isotopes**. The protons and neutrons make up the positively charged nucleus and the electrons move around the nucleus. Elements with similar chemical properties, i.e. in the same group, have similar outer electron arrangements, e.g. lithium 2,1 and sodium 2,8,1. Metals are found on the left-hand side of the Periodic Table and non-metals on the right-hand side.

Metals form neutral or alkaline oxides on burning and non-metals form acidic oxides. Metals form positive ions, e.g. Na^+, and non-metals form negative ions, e.g. Cl^-.

Some elements burn in oxygen to form oxides which can show both acidic and alkaline properties, depending upon the conditions. For example, aluminium oxide and zinc oxide show both properties and are called **amphoteric oxides**. Aluminium oxide dissolves with difficulty in hydrochloric acid and dissolves in sodium hydroxide solution to form sodium aluminate. In Unit 7 you will see that we use the fact that aluminium oxide dissolves in sodium hydroxide as part of the test for aluminium ions.

Whether a substance is acidic, alkaline or neutral can be shown using an indicator. Universal Indicator changes colour a number of times and depending upon the colour it is possible to give the pH. A pH of 7 is neutral, less than 7 acidic and greater than 7 alkaline. When an alkali is added to an acid, a process of **neutralization** takes place.

A neutralization reaction is often represented by the ionic equation

$$H^+ + OH^- \rightarrow H_2O$$

Salts are produced by a process of neutralization, e.g. sodium chloride

$$NaOH + HCl \rightarrow NaCl + H_2O$$

If you need to revise this subject more thoroughly, see the relevant topics in the Letts GCSE *Science Study Guide*.

QUESTIONS

1 The Periodic Table may help you answer some parts of this question.

(a) The diagram below shows the structure of sodium chloride.

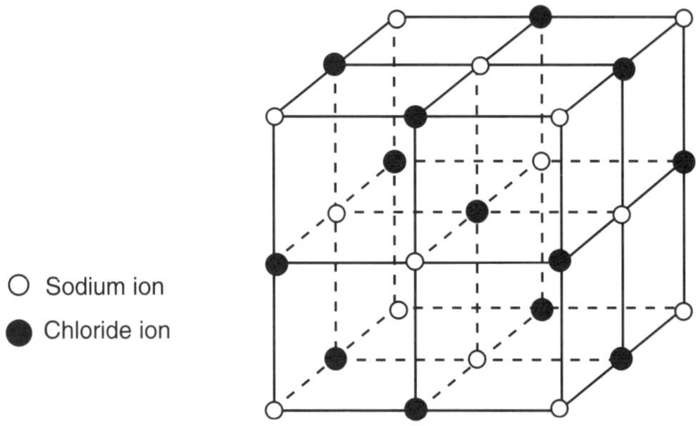

(i) How does the structure of a sodium ion differ from the structure of a sodium atom?

....

.... (1)

(ii) How does the structure of a chloride ion differ from the structure of a chlorine atom?

....

.... (1)

(iii) What type of chemical bond is present in sodium chloride?

.... (1)

(b) Use the diagram of sodium chloride to help you explain why:

(i) sodium chloride crystals can be cube shaped;

....

.... (1)

(ii) solid sodium chloride has a high melting point;

....

....

.... (2)

(iii) solid sodium chloride is an electrical insulator;

....

....

.... (2)

(iv) molten sodium chloride will undergo electrolysis;

....

....

.... (2)

SEG 1995

2 Temperature probes were used to record the surface temperature of the metal body of Concorde. The graph shows the results obtained.

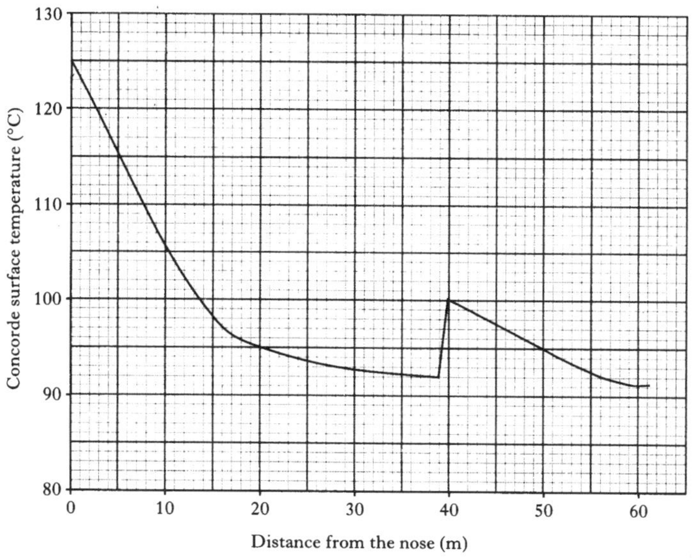

(a) In general, what happens to the surface temperature as the distance from the nose increases?

.... (1)

(b) At what distance from the nose is there a result which does not follow this general trend?

.... (1)

SEB 1993

3 (a) Use the Periodic Table to help you describe:

(i) the structure of a potassium (K) atom which has a mass number of 39;

....

....

QUESTIONS

....

....

....

.... (4)

(ii) why potassium (K) is more reactive than calcium (Ca);

....

....

....

.... (2)

(iii) why bromine (Br) is a more reactive non-metal than selenium (Se).

....

....

....

.... (2)

(b) From your knowledge of trends in the Periodic Table, predict how barium (Ba) reacts with water.

....

....

....

.... (2)

SEG 1994

4 A compound called ammonium ethanoate can be prepared by mixing ammonia solution (ammonium hydroxide) with dilute ethanoic acid. One molecule of ammonium hydroxide reacts with one molecule of acid. Ammonia solution has a pH of 10. A solution of ammonium ethanoate has a pH of 7. The table below shows the change in pH when ammonia solution is added to 20 cm^3 dilute ethanoic acid.

Vol of ammonia solution added (cm^3)	0	5	10	15	20	25
pH	3	3.5	5	8.5	X	9.5

(a) (i) Plot a line graph of volume of ammonia solution against pH using the axes given below.

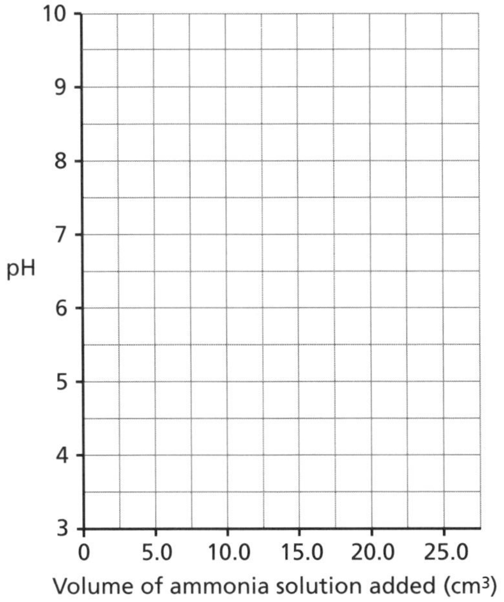

(4)

(ii) From your graph, find the volume of acid needed to produce a pH of 7.

.... (1)

(iii) From your graph, find the pH when an equal volume of ammonia solution (20.0 cm^3) had been added to the acid.

.... (1)

(iv) Using your answers to parts (ii) and (iii) above, do you think the concentration of ammonia solution was greater than, equal to or less than the concentration of the ethanoic acid?

....

.... (2)

(b) Complete the word equation below and, in the spaces provided beneath the equation, label the types of substances involved in the reaction.

ammonium hydroxide + ethanoic acid = ammonium ethanoate + ...

.... ACID .... (3)

(c) Name a suitable piece of laboratory apparatus for measuring out 20.0 cm^3 of dilute ethanoic acid.

.... (1)

ULEAC 1994

6 Explanation of the properties of materials

REVISION SUMMARY

There are three states of matter – **solid**, **liquid** and **gas**. All matter can exist in any of these states depending upon conditions of temperature and pressure. In all three states the material is made up of particles.

In a solid the particles are vibrating about fixed positions. If the solid is crystalline the particles are regularly arranged and usually closely packed. In a liquid the particles are still close together, but there is no regular arrangement. There is more movement of particles and the movement gets more as the temperature rises. In the gas state the particles have broken away from each other and are free to move around.

When a change of state occurs, e.g. solid to liquid, there is an associated energy change. In this case energy is required to break up the solid structure and give the particles additional kinetic energy. The reverse process – liquid to solid – will release energy. **Diffusion** is the movement of particles to spread out and fill all of the available space. Diffusion takes place rapidly with gases because the particles in a gas are moving rapidly. Diffusion takes place more slowly in liquids and solids because there is less movement of particles.

The relationship between pressure, temperature and volume of a fixed mass of gas is given by the relationship

$$\frac{p_1V_1}{T_1} = \frac{p_2V_2}{T_2}$$

where p, V and T refer to pressure, volume and absolute temperature.

Elements are made up of atoms. A piece of iron is made up solely of iron atoms. In a **mixture** there will be different types of atoms and the atoms of the different elements are not joined. In a **compound** again there will be atoms of different elements, but they are joined together. A mixture of hydrogen and oxygen can consist of hydrogen and oxygen in different proportions, but water, a compound of hydrogen and oxygen, always contains twice as many atoms of hydrogen as oxygen. Groups of atoms in elements or compounds are called **molecules**. An oxygen molecule consists of a pair of oxygen atoms together, O_2, and a water molecule is two hydrogen atoms and one oxygen atom, H_2O.

The properties of a material are related to the structure of the material. If the material is made up of molecules it will have low melting and boiling points. If it is made up of a giant structure of atoms or ions, it will have a high melting point. A giant structure of ions produces a melt which conducts electricity.

A radioactive material can produce three types of radiation – alpha, beta and gamma.

Alpha radiation consists of helium nuclei and is therefore positively charged. It is the least penetrating of the three types of radiation. It is deflected by magnetic fields. Beta radiation consists of a stream of electrons and is therefore negatively charged. It is more penetrating and more deflected by magnetic fields than alpha radiation. Gamma radiation is the most penetrating. It is high energy electromagnetic radiation and is not deflected by magnetic fields. The half-life of a radioactive isotope is the time taken for half of the radioactive atoms to decay or for the radioactive count to fall to half its original value.

When chemical bonds are broken energy is used, and energy is produced when bonds are formed. If a reaction is exothermic (gives out energy) the energy produced by the bonds formed is greater than the energy required to break the bonds.

If you need to revise this subject more thoroughly, see the relevant topics in the *Letts GCSE Science Study Guide.*

QUESTIONS

1 The diagrams show simple representations of hydrogen and bromine.

(a) In these diagrams, in which state are hydrogen and bromine?

.... (1)

(b) What do each of the following diagrams represent? Add suitable captions to the diagrams.

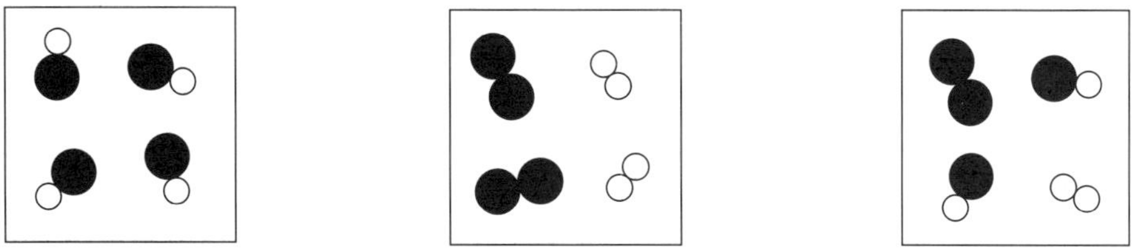

....

....

....

....

.... (3)

(c) (i) Draw a diagram to show the bonding in a hydrogen bromide gas molecule. Show only the outer electrons. What type of bonding is present in the molecule? (3)

Type of bonding ....

(ii) A damp thermometer is placed into a gas jar containing dry hydrogen bromide gas. The temperature shown on the thermometer rises. Suggest what changes occur to the hydrogen bromide when water is added.

....

QUESTIONS

....

....

.... (3)

2 Sue goes to check the pressure of the air in her car tyres. The manufacturer recommends a pressure of 200 kPa.
She finds that one tyre has a pressure of 180 kPa.

(a) Explain, in terms of moving particles, how air exerts a pressure in a car tyre.

....

....

.... (2)

(b) She drives to a garage and checks the same tyre again. Now the pressure is 190 kPa. Explain the difference, assuming that both pressure gauges are accurate.

....

....

.... (2)

(c) Doubling the pressure of a fixed mass of gas at constant temperature halves the volume.

(i) The table gives data about the pressure and volume of a fixed mass of gas at 300 K. Complete the table.

Pressure/kPa	50	100		400
Volume/dm^3	8	4	2	

(1)

(ii) Plot the data on the grid and draw a smooth curve through the points. (2)

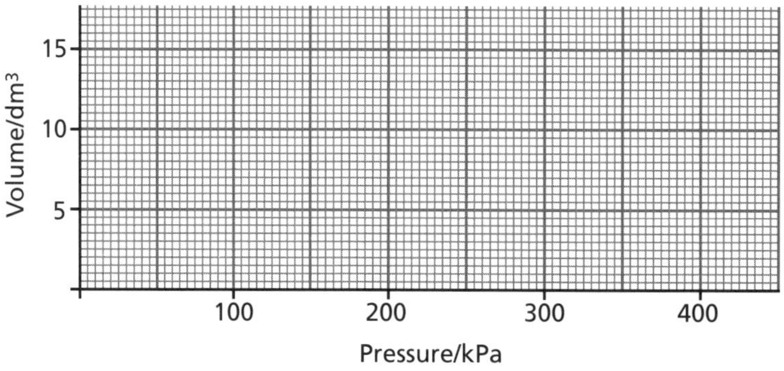

Letts Q&A

(iii) Calculate the pressure of the same mass of gas at 400 K assuming the volume is unchanged at 8 dm^3.

....

....

.... (3)

MEG 1994

3 An Investigation To Find Out Which Material is Best for Making Nuclear Waste Drums

Method

❶ Four nuclear waste drums of identical shape and size were constructed. Two drums were made of Zinctox alloy and two were made from Nicad alloy. For each alloy, the two drums were made with walls of different thicknesses.

❷ Equal amounts of nuclear waste were put into the four drums and the tops of the drums were sealed.

❸ The radiation escaping through the side of each drum was measured by holding a radiation meter at a distance of 1 metre from the drum.

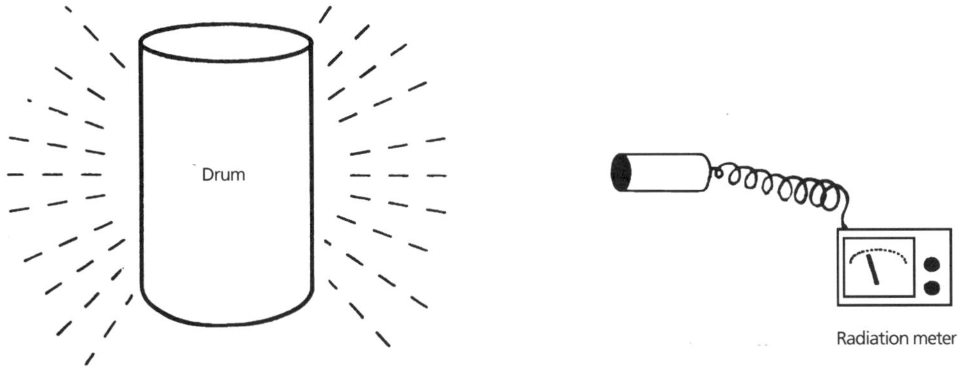

Results

Drum alloy	Thickness of wall (mm)	Radiation escaping (cpm)
Zinctox	50	650
Zinctox	100	540
Nicad	50	530
Nicad	100	390

(a) What **two** conclusions can be drawn from this experiment?

Conclusion 1 ....

....

Conclusion 2 ....

.... (3)

QUESTIONS

(b) Give **two** reasons why drums of radioactive waste may be stored deep underground.

Reason 1 ....

....

Reason 2 ....

.... (2)

SEB 1993

4 Copper is a dense, ductile (that is, can be drawn out into a wire) metal with a high resistance to corrosion. Aluminium bronze is an alloy of copper and aluminium. This alloy has the same resistance to corrosion as copper but its greatest strength is twice the strength of pure copper. The greatest strength is obtained when the alloy contains 10 per cent of aluminium by mass.

(a) **Sketch** on the axes provided below, a graph to show how the strength of aluminium bronze changes with composition. (1)

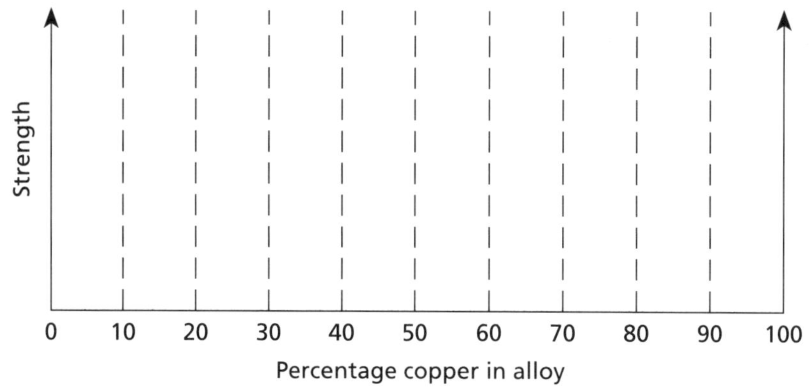

(b) The diagram below shows the arrangement of atoms in pure copper metal.

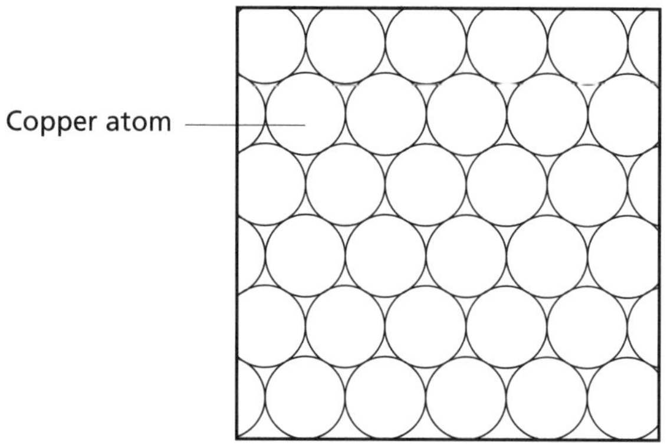

Use the diagram above to help you **explain** why copper metal

(i) is dense;

....

....

....

.... (2)

(ii) is ductile.

....

....

....

.... (2)

(c) (i) In the space provided below draw a labelled diagram to show the arrangement of atoms in aluminium bronze. (2)

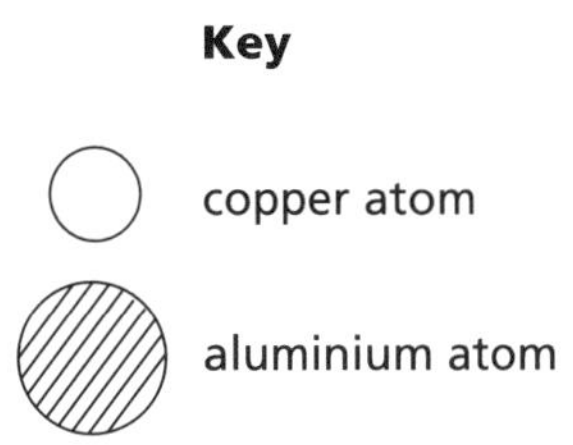

(ii) Use your completed diagram to help you explain why aluminium bronze is much stronger than pure copper.

....

....

.... (2)

(iii) Suggest **one** use of aluminium bronze. State the reason why aluminium bronze is used for the purpose you have suggested.

....

.... (2)

SEG 1994

7 Chemical changes

REVISION SUMMARY

Changes which take place when materials are heated or cooled may be **temporary** (e.g. freezing water) or **permanent** (burning wood). If they are temporary they can easily be reversed.

Many natural materials (limestone, marble, wood) have a wide range of uses. Other materials (steel, glass, aluminium, cement) are made from raw materials by chemical reactions.

Rusting of iron and steel and combustion (burning) of materials involve reactions with oxygen. They are **oxidation** processes. Rusting also requires water to be present. Combustion involves the burning of a material in oxygen to form one or more **oxides**.

E.g. magnesium + oxygen → magnesium oxide

This is a **word equation** which summarizes the reaction. Magnesium and oxygen are **reactants**; magnesium oxide is a **product**. The same reaction can be represented by a **symbolic equation**.

E.g. $2Mg(s) + O_2(g) \rightarrow 2MgO(s)$

Chemical reactions which release energy are called **exothermic** reactions and reactions which take in energy are called **endothermic** reactions. These can be represented in energy level diagrams.

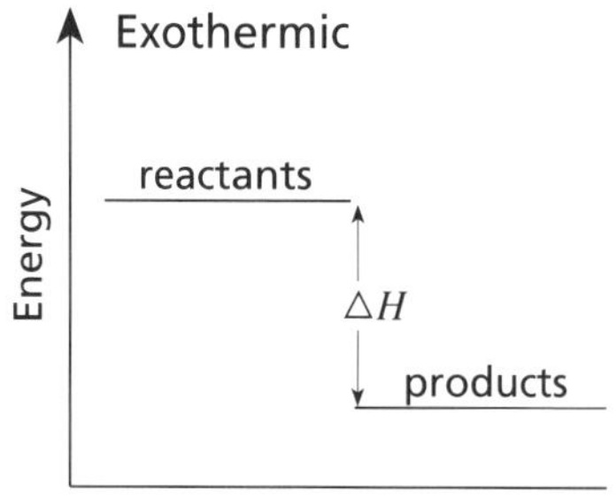

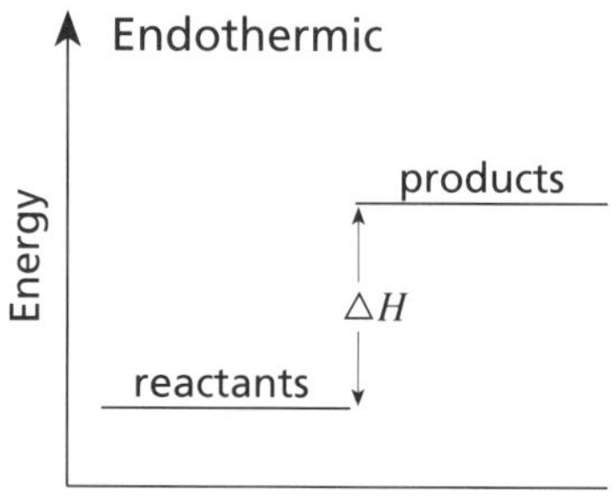

Factors which speed up the rate of a chemical reaction include:

- Increasing temperature.
- Increasing the concentration of one or more of the reactants.
- Using a **catalyst**.
- Using one of the reactants in a more finely powdered form which increases the surface area of a solid.
- Light.
- Pressure for reactions involving gases.

Most metals react with oxygen, water and acids, but at different rates. Metals are often arranged in order of reactivity, called a **reactivity series**. Such a series is:

K Na Ca Mg Al Zn Fe Pb Cu Ag

→ decreasing reactivity

A reactivity series can be used to predict the products of a chemical reaction.

E.g. copper(II) sulphate + iron → copper + iron(II) sulphate

A reaction takes place because iron is more reactive than copper (higher in the reactivity series).

Electrolysis involves the **decomposition** of an **electrolyte** using electricity. Electrolysis takes place when ions are free to move when an electrolyte is molten or dissolved in water. The products of electrolysis are formed at the electrodes.

E.g. lead(II) bromide (molten) → lead (formed at the negative electrode, called the **cathode**) + bromine (formed at the positive electrode, called the **anode**)

Metals and hydrogen are usually produced at the cathode, and oxygen or one of the halogens at the anode. **Ionic** equations are often used to represent changes taking place at the electrodes.

Cathode: $Pb^{2+} + 2e^- \rightarrow Pb$ Anode: $2Br^- \rightarrow Br_2 + 2e^-$

If you need to revise this subject more thoroughly, see the relevant topics in the *Letts GCSE Science Study Guide.*

Letts Q&A

1 The diagram summarizes how some important materials can be made from methane.

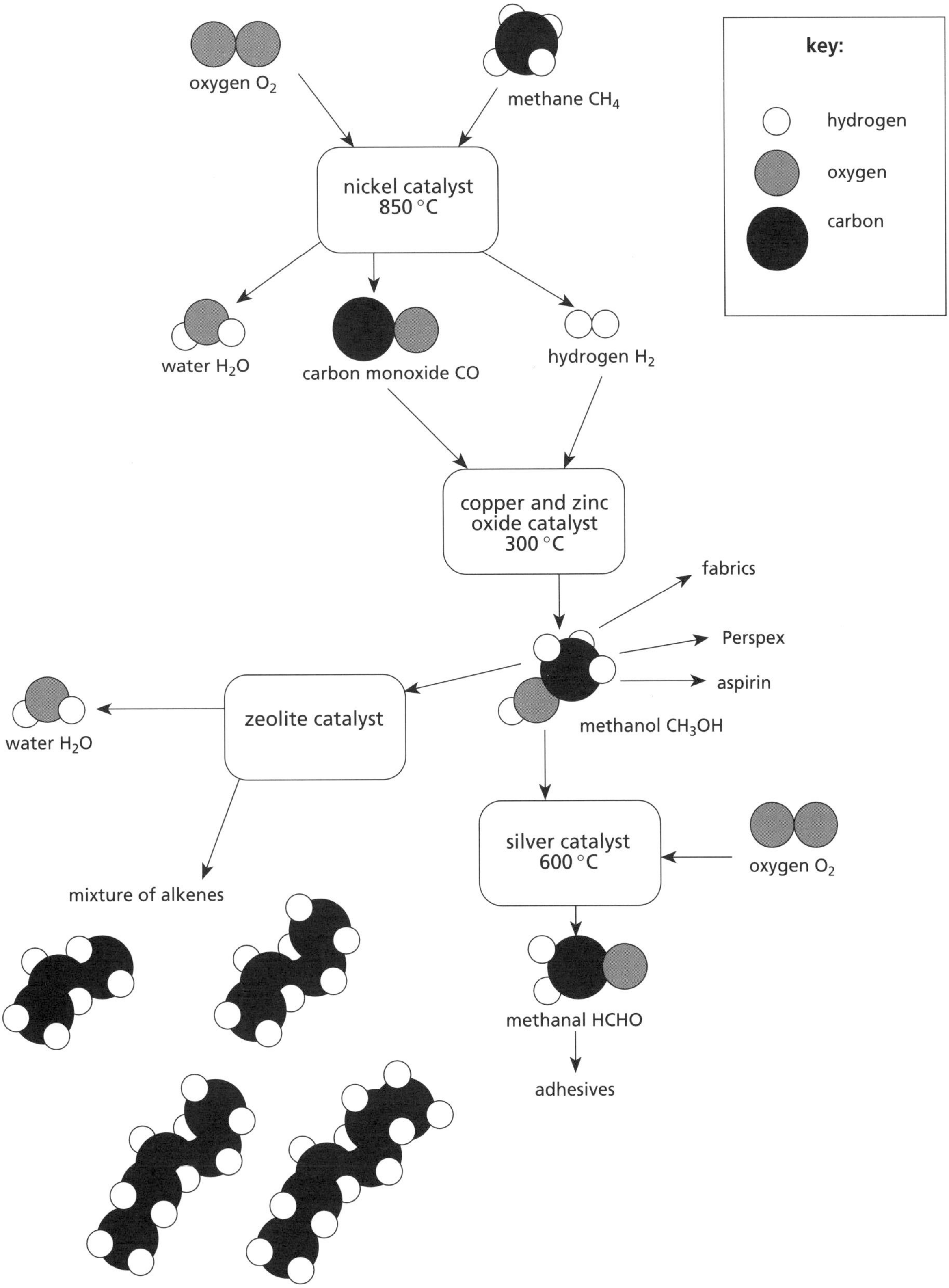

(a) What is an important source of methane for industry?

.... (1)

QUESTIONS

(b) The nickel catalyst has to be heated to 850 °C to start the reaction between oxygen and methane. After this, heating is not necessary and the catalyst reaction remains unchanged. What does this suggest about the reaction of methane and oxygen?

.... (1)

(c) What type of reaction is the conversion of methanol into methanal?

.... (1)

(d) A zeolite structure is very open with lots of tiny holes through it. Why does this help a zeolite to be a good catalyst?

.... (1)

(e) Write a balanced symbolic equation for the formation of methanol.

.... (2)

(f) Suggest a use for the mixture of alkenes produced.

.... (1)

2 Aluminium is manufactured by passing electricity through a molten mixture containing aluminium oxide, Al_2O_3. The electrolysis is carried out in cells lined with carbon which forms the negative electrode (cathode). Carbon rods are used as positive electrodes (anodes). Bauxite, the ore of aluminium, is imported into the British Isles. The production of aluminium requires very large amounts of electricity.

(a) (i) Write a balanced equation, including electrons, for the reaction producing aluminium at the negative electrode (cathode).

.... (1)

(ii) One cell produces 500 kg of aluminium per day. Calculate the mass of aluminium oxide used by the cell each day. (Relative atomic masses, A_r: Al = 27, O = 16)

....

....

....

.... (3)

(b) Suggest and explain **two** economic or environmental points to consider when deciding where to build a new aluminium plant.

First point: ....

....

....

Second point: ....

....

.... (4)

(c) To produce 1 mole of aluminium metal by electrolysis needs 289 500 coulombs of electric charge. Explain why it only needs 193 000 coulombs to liberate 1 mole of lead.

....

....

.... (2)

MEG 1994

3 When a lump of marble is put into hydrochloric acid, carbon dioxide gas is formed.

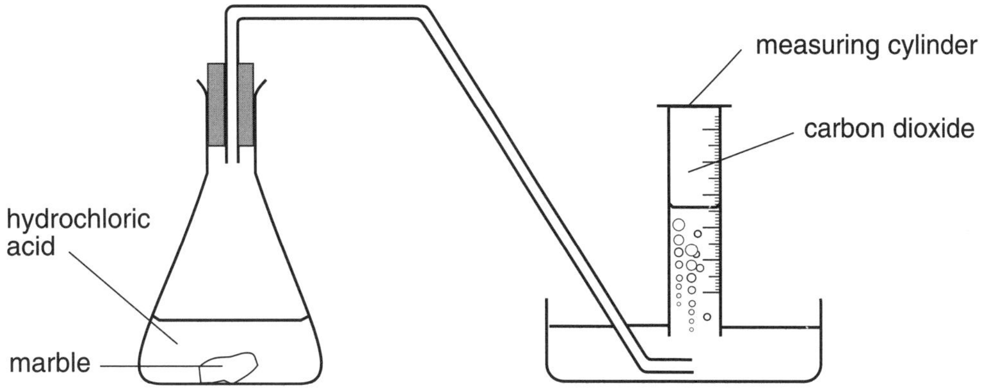

The graph overleaf shows the total volume of carbon dioxide formed at different times.

Most of the marble is left at the end of the experiment.

QUESTIONS

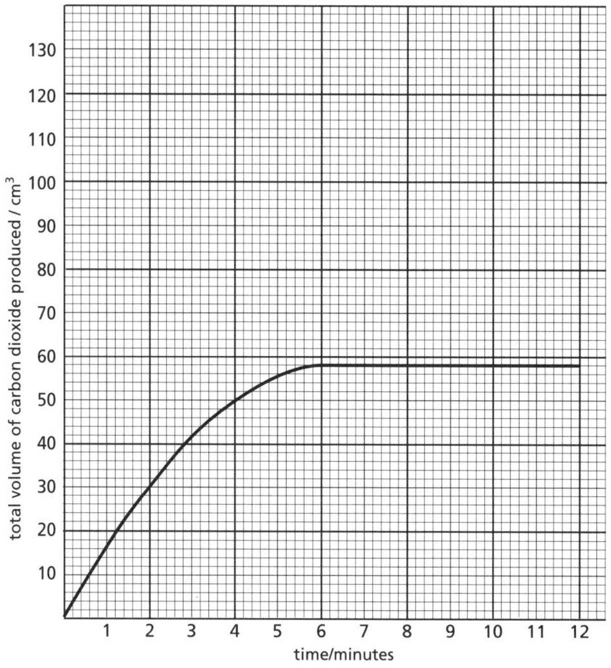

(a) What is the total volume of carbon dioxide formed by the end of the reaction?

.... (2)

(b) When is the reaction quickest? Tick **one** box only.

☐ 0–2 mins ☐ 2–4 mins

☐ 4–6 mins ☐ 6–8 mins

Explain your answer.

.... (2)

(c) The experiment is done again.
The quantity of marble is the same.
The temperature is the same as in the first experiment.
Double the volume of the same acid is used.
Most of the marble is left at the end of the experiment.

On the graph, sketch the shape of the graph you would expect this time. (2)

(d) The reaction mixture could be changed to increase the rate of the reaction.
For each change below explain clearly in terms of the particles present why the rate of the reaction is increased.

(i) Increasing the concentration of the acid.

....

.... (2)

(ii) Increasing the temperature.

....

.... (2)

(iii) Breaking the marble into smaller pieces.

....

.... (2)

(e) The equation for the reaction between hydrochloric acid (HCl) and marble ($CaCO_3$) is

$$CaCO_3 + 2HCl \rightarrow CaCl_2 + CO_2 + H_2O$$

Calculate the mass of carbon dioxide produced from 5.0 g of calcium carbonate. Show your working clearly.

The relative atomic mass (A_r) of calcium is 40.
The relative atomic mass (A_r) of carbon is 12.
The relative atomic mass (A_r) of oxygen is 16.
The relative atomic mass (A_r) of hydrogen is 1.
The relative atomic mass (A_r) of chlorine is 35.5.

....

....

....

Answer: ....g (3)

MEG 1995

4 Two pieces of steel can be joined together by Thermit welding.
This is carried out by placing a mixture of aluminium and iron(III) oxide between two pieces to be welded. The process is started by lighting a fuse of magnesium ribbon. The reaction between aluminium and iron(III) oxide is sufficiently exothermic to melt the iron produced, which then welds the two pieces of steel together.

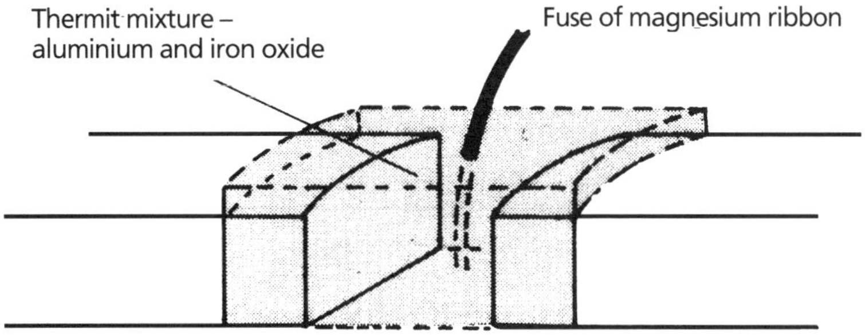

The equation for the reaction is

$$2Al + Fe_2O_3 \rightarrow Al_2O_3 + 2Fe$$

QUESTIONS

(a) Explain, in terms of bonds, why this reaction is exothermic.

....

....

....

....

.... (3)

(b) Sketch and label an energy level diagram, showing the relative positions of reactants and products, for the reaction between aluminium and iron(III) oxide.

(3)

(c) Explain why a fuse of burning magnesium is needed in Thermit welding.

....

....

....

.... (3)

(d) Give TWO safety precautions which should be taken during Thermit welding and explain the reasons for the precautions.

1: ....

....

2: ....

.... (2)

ULEAC 1994

REVISION SUMMARY

There are three parts which make up the Earth – the **crust**, the **mantle** and the **core**. The crust is a thin layer of surface rocks, between 7 km and 40 km thick. Underneath the crust is the mantle and in the centre of the Earth is the core. Our understanding of the structure of the core comes from studies including the passage of sound waves through the earth. These studies, called seismic studies, show scientists that the inner core of the Earth is solid.

The work of Alfred Wegener (1880–1930) showed that the Earth's crust is made up from a number of huge **plates** which are floating on the liquid magma. Originally the plates made up one supercontinent called the Pangaea. These plates are moving very slowly – perhaps only a few centimetres a year. The movement of these plates is called **plate tectonics**.

Where two plates are sliding past each other, they produce stresses and strains which may be released suddenly in an **earthquake**. When two plates are moving apart, a crack will appear in the Earth's crust. Molten rock from the mantle will come to the surface and new rocks will be formed. This often takes place under oceans and is not easily seen. This is called a **constructive plate margin**.

When two plates collide, rocks are squeezed together. This causes the pushing of one plate upwards to create a mountain range. The Himalayas were formed from the collision of the Eurasian and Indian plates. Alternatively one of the plates is pushed back downwards into the magma. This is called a **destructive plate margin**.

The rocks of the earth can be classified as igneous, metamorphic and sedimentary.

- **Igneous rocks** are formed when molten magma from inside the Earth is cooled. They are crystalline and the size of the crystals depend upon the rate of cooling. Large crystals are formed when the cooling is slow. There are two types of igneous rocks – **intrusive** rocks (e.g. granite), which are formed inside the Earth, and **extrusive** rocks (e.g. basalt), which are formed on the surface of the Earth.
- **Metamorphic rocks** are formed when high temperatures and pressures act on sedimentary and igneous rocks. Marble is a metamorphic rock produced from limestone.
- **Sedimentary rocks** are formed when rocks in the Earth are eroded and the sediments are transported and deposited. When these layers of rock fragments are compressed over a long period, sedimentary rocks are formed. Chalk is a sedimentary rock.

Rocks are being continuously recycled in the rock cycle.

NORMAL COMPOSITION OF DRY AIR (by volume)

nitrogen	78.1%
oxygen	21.0%
argon	0.9%
carbon dioxide	0.03%
Traces of	neon krypton xenon

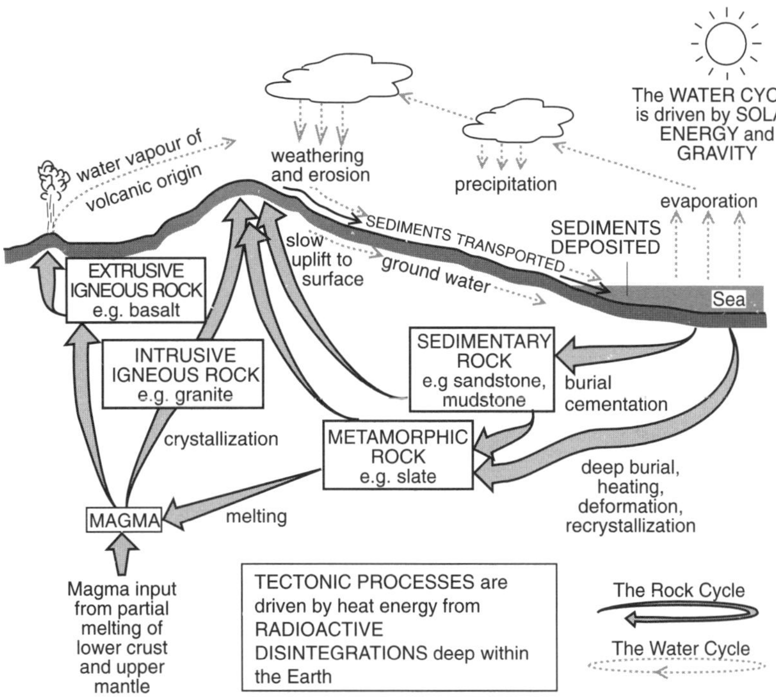

If you need to revise this subject more thoroughly, see the relevant topics in the Letts GCSE Science Study Guide.

Letts Q&A

QUESTIONS

1 The table below shows the density of the Earth and of different types of rock from which it is composed.

Type of rock	Density (kg/m^3)
Crustal rock	2 800
Mantle rock	4 200
Average overall density of Earth	5 500

(a) Explain what evidence can be obtained from these readings about the nature of the Earth's core.

....

....

....

.... (2)

(b) The table below gives information about three types of earthquake wave.

Type of wave	Relative speed	Passes through	Travels
L	very slow	solids	around the crust
P	fast	solids and liquids	through the Earth
S	medium	solids only	through the Earth

The diagram below shows the Earth's core, mantle and crust. There has been an earthquake at point E. S_1, S_2, S_3 and S_4 are seismograph stations.

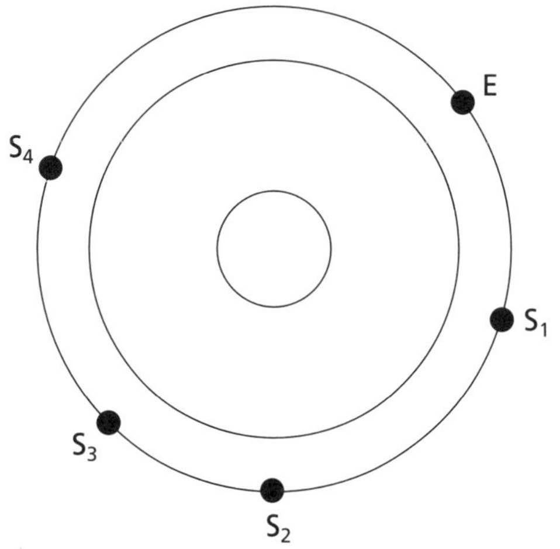

(i) Which station would receive only two of these types of wave? Give a reason for your answer.

....

QUESTIONS

....

.... (2)

(ii) Which station is likely to receive waves from the earthquake first?
Give a reason for your answer.

....

....

.... (2)

(c) The map below shows the boundaries of the Earth's plates.

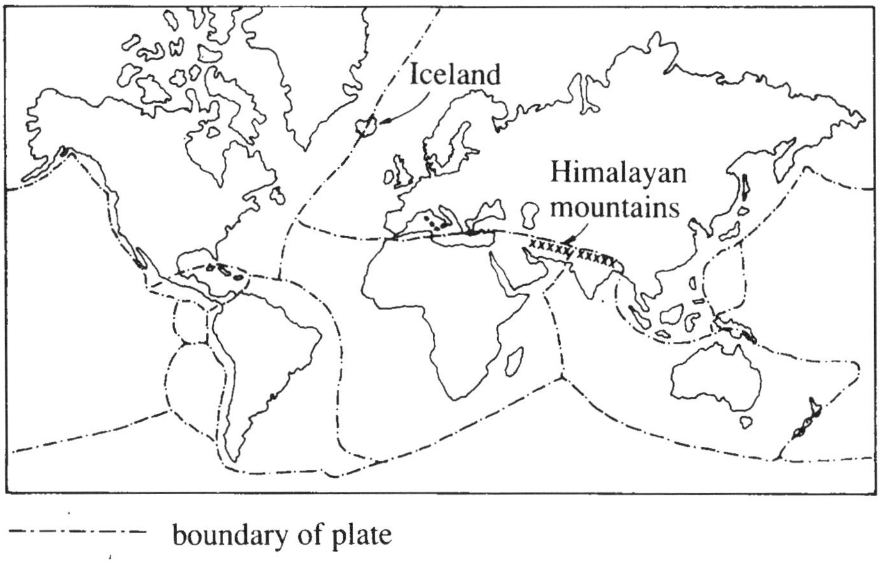

Use the map to answer the following questions.

(i) Explain why the island of Iceland consists almost completely of igneous rock.

....

....

....

....

.... (3)

QUESTIONS

(ii) Describe how the Himalayan mountains were formed.

....

.... (2)

ULEAC 1994

2 An underwater ridge called the Mid-Atlantic Ridge runs along the floor of the Atlantic Ocean. The age of the oldest sea floor sediments has been estimated at different distances from this ridge. The table below shows the results.

Distance from ridge/km	Age of oldest sediments/millions of years
250	10
500	26
750	38
1500	75

(a) Use this information to plot a graph showing how the age of the oldest sediments on the floor of the Atlantic Ocean depends on the distance from the Mid-Atlantic Ridge. (4)

You will need a square piece of graph paper (80 small squares on x and y axes)

(b) (i) Explain how the graph can be used to estimate the rate at which the ocean floor has spread apart in the past.

....

....

.... (1)

(ii) Use your graph to estimate the age of the oldest sediments 1000 km from the ridge.

....

.... (1)

(c) The spreading apart of the ocean floor on either side of the ridge can be explained by the theory of plate tectonics. According to the theory, materials near the ridge move as shown in the diagram.

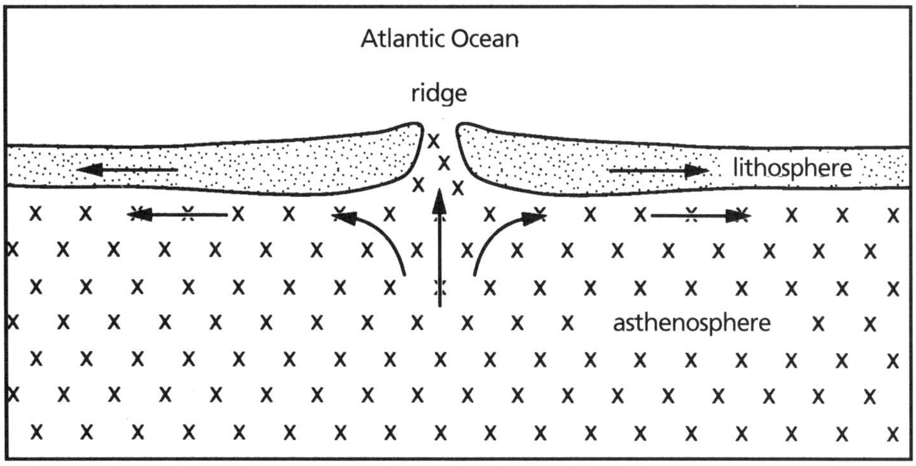

How can the theory of plate tectonics explain the formation of volcanoes at ocean ridges?

....

....

....

.... (4)

(d) A link has been suggested between the extinction of dinosaurs and a decrease in volcanic activity about 65 million years ago. Volcanoes release large quantities of carbon dioxide gas.
Suggest why scientists believe this change might have led to the extinction of dinosaurs.

....

....

....

.... (2)

MEG 1994

9 Electricity and magnetism

REVISION SUMMARY

Logic gates are electronically operated switches. With the exception of the NOT gate, most common logic gates have two inputs. The name of the gate describes the conditions of the inputs for the output to be 'on', or at logic 1.

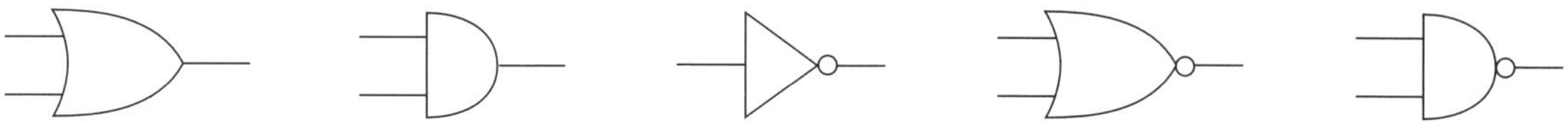

Note that NOR stands for NOT OR; it is the same as an OR gate followed by a NOT. Similarly, NAND acts as an AND gate followed by a NOT.

Logic gates are often used with **sensors**, such as light, temperature and moisture sensors, to switch things on or off according to environmental conditions. These electronic systems often involve the use of **feedback**, where the output of the system feeds back to the input. An example of this is temperature control.

Useful circuits can be made by combining logic gates. The bistable circuit is a memory circuit; it 'remembers' the input signal (either 0 or 1) even when that input has been removed. The diagram represents a bistable unit.

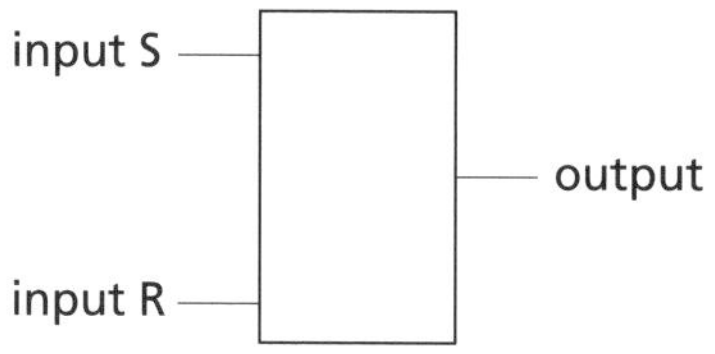

The binary digit (0 or 1) which is to be remembered is applied to the S (or set) input and this appears at the output. The output then keeps that value even when the input value is changed or removed. The R input is to reset the bistable so that it is ready to remember another digit. As well as being used in large numbers in computer memories, bistable circuits have applications as latches in circuits such as burglar alarms.

The amount of electric **current** passing in a circuit depends on the **potential difference** (p.d.), or **voltage**, and the **resistance**. Increasing the voltage applies a bigger force to the moving charges, giving a greater flow. Resistance is the opposition to the electric current; more resistance in the circuit reduces the current passing.
The formula for calculating resistance is:

$$\text{resistance} = \frac{\text{potential difference}}{\text{current}} \quad \text{or in symbols} \quad R = \frac{V}{I}$$

Resistance is measured in ohms (symbol Ω).

The job of a circuit is to transfer energy from the source, battery or power supply, to the components – lamps, heater, motors and other devices.

Potential difference, or voltage, is a measure of the energy transfer. A 12 V power supply transfers 12 joules of energy to each coulomb of **charge**. When the charge flows through a lamp the energy is transferred into heat energy and light energy. So potential difference measures energy transfer both ways – the p.d. across a power supply measures the electrical energy transfer **into** the circuit and the p.d. across a component measures the energy transfer **from** electrical energy.

Power measures the energy transfer each second; this is determined by both the current and the potential difference.

REVISION SUMMARY

The following equations show the relationships between current, charge, power and potential difference:

$$\text{current (in A)} = \frac{\text{charge flow (in C)}}{\text{time (in s)}}$$

$$\text{potential difference (in V)} = \frac{\text{energy transfer (in J)}}{\text{charge (in C)}}$$

$$\text{power (in W)} = \text{p.d. (in V)} \times \text{current (in A)}$$

Written in symbols, these are:

$$I = \frac{Q}{t} \qquad V = \frac{E}{Q} \qquad P = IV$$

Electric currents also have magnetic fields; this is called **electromagnetism** and is used in devices such as relays (electromagnetic switches), motors and loudspeakers to produce movement.

Electromagnetic induction is the name given to the way in which electrical energy is generated and transformed. In a generator or bicycle dynamo a magnet rotates inside a coil of wire. The changing magnetic field causes a voltage to be induced; the size of the induced voltage depends on the rate at which the magnetic field changes.

Transformers are efficient devices which use electromagnetism for changing the size of an alternating voltage. The equation for this is:

$$\frac{\text{number of turns on primary coil}}{\text{number of turns on secondary coil}} = \frac{\text{primary voltage}}{\text{secondary voltage}}$$

Transformers do not give a free supply of energy; when used to increase the voltage they reduce the current and they give increased currents when the voltage is reduced.

$$\frac{\text{number of turns on primary coil}}{\text{number of turns on secondary coil}} = \frac{\text{secondary current}}{\text{primary current}}$$

The electricity supply industry makes extensive use of transformers; transmitting energy at high voltages enables low currents to be used which reduces the energy losses in transmission. Transformers step up the voltage at the power station before the energy is fed into the grid and step down the voltage in several stages before the energy is delivered to homes, commerce and industry.

The joule is too small a unit for measuring the energy supplied to homes, so the electricity supply industry uses the kilowatt hour. The energy transferred is calculated using the formula:

$$\text{energy (in kWh)} = \text{power (in kW)} \times \text{time (in h)}$$

Electric appliances need to be fitted with safety features to reduce the risk of fire and electrocution. Fuses fitted in the consumer unit (or fuse box) should cut off the current if it reaches such a level that the wiring cables are in danger of overheating and being set on fire. In a similar way, fuses fitted to plugs protect from fire hazard. The fuse wire melts and this stops the current if there is a fault that causes a larger than normal current to pass.

Earth wires should be connected to the casing of any appliance that has a metal case. Should the case become 'live' a large current then passes to earth which 'blows' (melts) the fuse and cuts off the electrical supply.

Televisions and X-ray tubes both use high-speed beams of electrons produced by **thermionic emission**. In televisions the electron beam is directed to the desired part of the screen where it strikes fluorescent materials called phosphors. These convert some of the kinetic energy of the moving electrons into electromagnetic radiation in the visible spectrum, or light energy. X-ray tubes use higher energy electron beams which are fired at a metal target. The electromagnetic radiation produced has a higher energy than that from the phosphors in a television tube. This high-energy radiation is in the short wavelength part of the electromagnetic spectrum.

If you need to revise this subject more thoroughly, see the relevant topics in the *Letts GCSE Science Study Guide*.

Letts Q&A

QUESTIONS

1 Logic gates can be used to switch electrical devices on and off according to environmental conditions. An exterior lamp fitted to a house is controlled by logic gates. The inputs to the gates come from a light sensor and an infrared sensor. The tables show the inputs to the logic gates from the sensors.

Light condition	Input from light sensor
light	1
dark	0

Infrared condition	Input from infrared sensor
high	1
low	0

(a) What could cause the amount of infrared radiation to change from 'low' to 'high'?

.... (1)

(b) The diagram shows the circuit that is used.

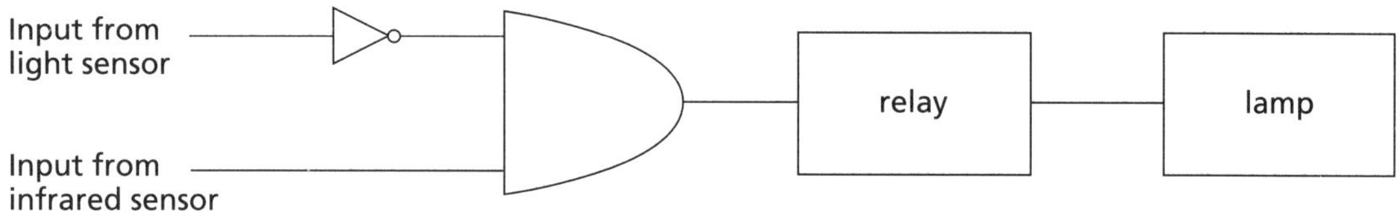

(i) Complete the table to show the state of the output from the AND gate.

Light condition	Infrared condition	AND gate output
dark	low	
light	high	
dark	high	
light	low	

(4)

(ii) Describe the conditions necessary for the lamp to be switched on.

....

....

.... (2)

(c) A householder wishes to use this circuit to switch on an outside lamp while he puts his car in the garage after returning home at night.

(i) Explain why the circuit shown in the diagram is not suitable for this purpose.

....

.... (1)

(ii) Describe and explain how a bistable circuit could be added to make the circuit suitable.

....

....

.... (3)

2 (a) A variable resistor can be used to change the amount of current passing in a circuit. The diagram shows a circuit that can be used to illuminate the instruments on a car dashboard.

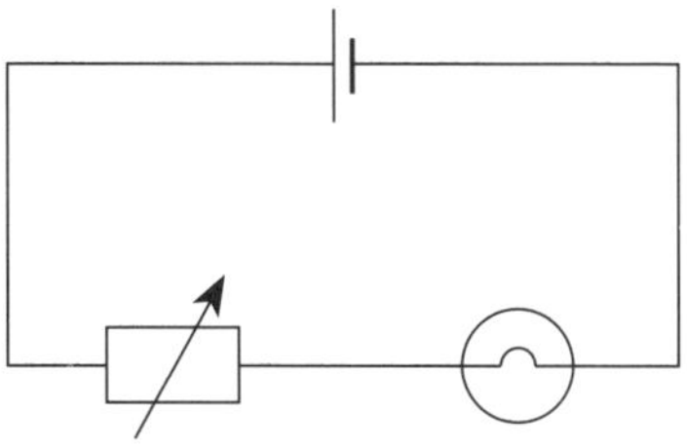

(i) Describe what the circuit is able to do.

.... (1)

(ii) Use words from the following list to complete the sentences.

current **greatest** **resistance** **smallest**

When the lamp is dim the .... of the variable resistor is at

its .... This causes the .... in the

lamp filament to be at its .... (4)

(b) When the lamp is operating at its normal brightness the potential difference across the filament is 12 V and the current passing is 0.2 A.

(i) Calculate the resistance of the filament at its normal brightness.

(3)

(ii) Calculate the power of the lamp at its normal brightness.

(3)

QUESTIONS

3 Loudspeakers use a combination of a fixed magnet and an electromagnet to produce movement of the paper cone.

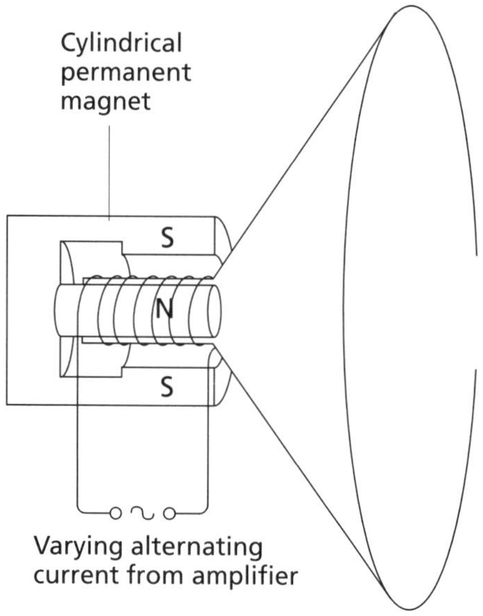

(a) Complete the diagram to show the magnetic field of the permanent magnet. (2)

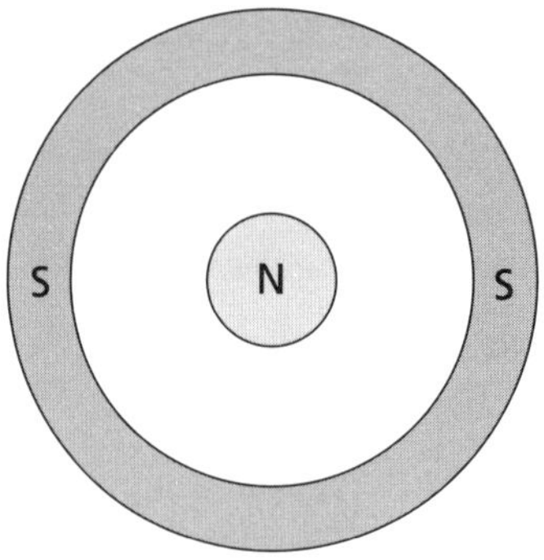

(b) Describe and explain how the paper cone moves when an alternating current passes in the coil of wire that is placed between the poles of the fixed magnet.

....

....

....

.... (4)

(c) Explain fully how the electric current transfers energy from the amplifier to the paper cone.

....

....

.... (3)

4 Many radios can work from either batteries or the mains electricity supply. A transformer is used to convert the mains voltage to the value needed by the radio. The transformer can be built into either the radio or the mains plug.

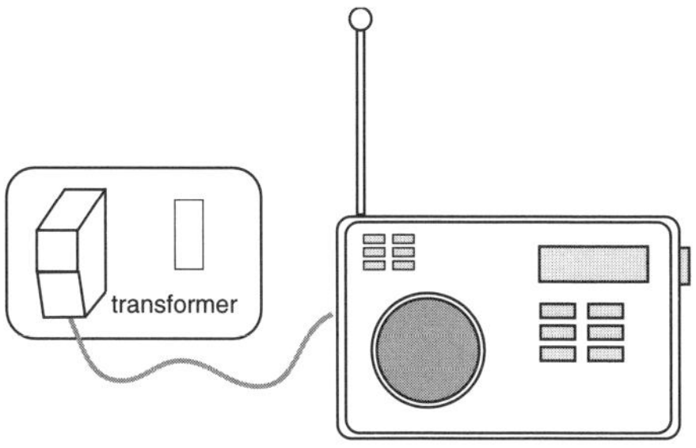

One radio has the following label printed on it.

Supply into transformer	240V	0.01A
Output from transformer	6V	0.35A
Battery operation	6V	0.3A

(a) (i) Give the formula that links the power of an electrical device, the potential difference (voltage) and the current.

.... (1)

(ii) Calculate the power when the radio is working from batteries.

....watts (2)

The transformer that is used to convert the mains voltage is made of two coils of wire wrapped around a soft iron core.

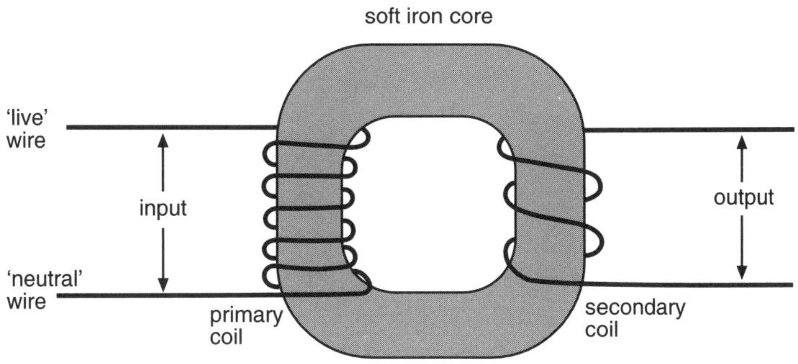

(b) Explain why a transformer will produce an output voltage when an a.c. supply is connected to the primary coil, but not when a d.c. supply is used.

....

.... (2)

(c) The input voltage to the primary coil is 240V. The output voltage from the secondary coil is 6V. If the primary coil has 8000 turns, how many turns must the secondary coil have?

....

.... (3)

MEG 1995

10 Energy resources and energy transfer

REVISION SUMMARY

For an object to have energy it must be able to make something happen. Fuels, things on the move, things that have been lifted up, electromagnetic radiation and materials transmitting sound or other vibrations all have energy.

The table lists the different forms of energy and gives a description of each one.

Form of energy	Description
Kinetic	Energy due to movement
Gravitational potential	Energy gained when an object is lifted up
Elastic potential	Energy stored when an object is stretched or deformed
Sound	Energy of the molecules transmitting the sound
Chemical	Energy stored by all foods and fuels; released when they are oxidized or undergo other exothermic reactions
Nuclear	Released as kinetic energy when a large nucleus splits up (fission) or a small nucleus is created from its constituent particles (fusion)
Thermal (heat)	The energy an object absorbs when its temperature rises and releases when its temperature falls; also absorbed or released when a substance changes state
Light	Energy of the visible part of the electromagnetic spectrum
Radiant	This term is sometimes used to describe the energy of any part of the electromagnetic spectrum
Electrical	The energy transferred to charged particles from a source of electricity
Magnetic	The energy in a magnetic field

Energy is constantly being transferred between these different forms. A braking car is transferring kinetic energy into thermal energy. When a car accelerates chemical energy from the fuel is being transferred into kinetic energy. However, a car travelling at a constant speed on the level is just transferring chemical energy into thermal energy of the surroundings!

Devices such as heaters, lamps, television sets and radios are designed to carry out a particular energy transfer; a gas fire is designed to transfer chemical energy from the gas into thermal energy and a lamp is designed to transfer electrical energy into light energy. Although all the energy that goes into one of these devices must come out (this is known as conservation of energy; the total amount of energy remains the same), it does not all come out in the desired form.

Tungsten filament lamps are poor at achieving the desired energy transfer, typically producing about 5 J of light energy for every 100 J of electrical energy supplied. The rest is emitted as thermal energy. Modern fluorescent lamps are more efficient; they transfer more of the energy input into the desired output, i.e. light. The efficiency of a device is the fraction or percentage of the energy input that is output in a useful form. Filament lamps have an efficiency of about 5%, while that for fluorescent lamps is about 20%.

There are three mechanisms by which thermal energy from hot objects such as lamps and heaters is lost to the surroundings.

❶ Everything emits infrared **radiation**: the rate of emission increases with increasing temperature and also depends on the nature of the surface. A dull, dark surface emits more radiation than a shiny one at the same temperature. The dark surface is also a better absorber than the shiny one; aluminium foil and silvered surfaces are used as insulators because they reflect infrared radiation so they can reduce the amount leaving a hot object or entering a cold one.

❷ **Conduction** is the transfer of energy from an energetic molecule to a less energetic one when they collide. Conduction in metals is a more rapid process than in non-metals because the free electrons diffuse within the metal, spreading the energy around.

REVISION SUMMARY

❸ **Convection** currents only occur in fluids (liquids and gases); they are caused by differences in density when part of the fluid is warmed or cooled. Convection currents keep the air circulating in a refrigerator and in a room that is heated by a 'radiator'.

Energy lost to the surroundings by a hot object cannot be recovered easily. This is because it becomes spread out and raises the temperature of the surroundings by a very small amount. It is not easy to extract energy from a low-temperature source; one way in which it can be done is by using a heat pump. This device is like a refrigerator running in reverse, with the energy absorber (the ice box in a refrigerator) being placed outside, often underground or in a river, and the energy emitter (the cooling pipes at the back of a refrigerator) inside a building.

The amount of energy absorbed or released when an object heats up or cools down depends on the temperature change, the quantity of material and its specific heat capacity. The specific heat capacity is the energy transfer needed to change the temperature of 1 kg of material by 1 °C or 1 K. The equation is:

$$\text{energy change} = \text{mass} \times \text{specific heat capacity} \times \text{temperature change}$$

Most of the energy that we transfer in our homes comes from **fossil fuels**: energy from the Sun was trapped millions of years ago and stored as chemical energy. Fossil fuels are **non-renewable**; we cannot make any more coal, gas or oil. Nuclear fission fuels such as uranium are also non-renewable. Some electricity is generated from renewable sources; hydroelectric power uses energy from the Sun that drives the water cycle, and wind power uses energy from the Sun that causes movement of airstreams. Solar cells convert energy from the Sun directly into electrical energy, but their high cost and low efficiency give them limited use in the UK.

Our bodies use **renewable energy sources**: plants transfer energy from the Sun into chemical energy; unlike the formation of coal, this is a short-term process and one that can be repeated many times in a short time scale.

Cost is an important factor when choosing an energy source and this is often governed by availability. Environmental factors are increasingly being taken into account. Whereas wind 'farms' do not cause the atmospheric pollution associated with fossil fuels, some people regard them as being noisy and ugly. Social factors to be taken into account include employment and environmental changes that could affect tourism or the livelihood of a community.

If you need to revise this subject more thoroughly, see the relevant topics in the *Letts GCSE Science Study Guide.*

QUESTIONS

1 Choose energy types from the following list

Chemical **Electrical** **Gravitational potential**
Kinetic **Light** **Sound** **Thermal**

to describe the **main** energy transfer that takes place in each of the following processes.

(a) A bus setting off from a bus stop.

.... energy to .... energy. (2)

(b) A skier speeding up as she skis downhill.

.... energy to .... energy. (2)

(c) A mains-operated radio playing music.

.... energy to .... energy. (2)

(d) A gas fire heating a room.

.... energy to .... energy. (2)

2 Although most of the electrical energy generated in the UK comes from burning fossil fuels such as coal, oil and gas, a significant amount is generated using moving water; this is called 'hydroelectric power'.

(a) Write down **three** advantages of using hydroelectric power instead of burning fossil fuels.

....

....

.... (3)

(b) What is the energy source for hydroelectric power ?

.... (1)

(c) In a pumped storage system, water is pumped from a low reservoir to a high one at night when there is little demand for electricity. The water can be released, generating electricity as it goes back to the low reservoir, in order to satisfy peak demand. The diagram shows the arrangement of the reservoirs.

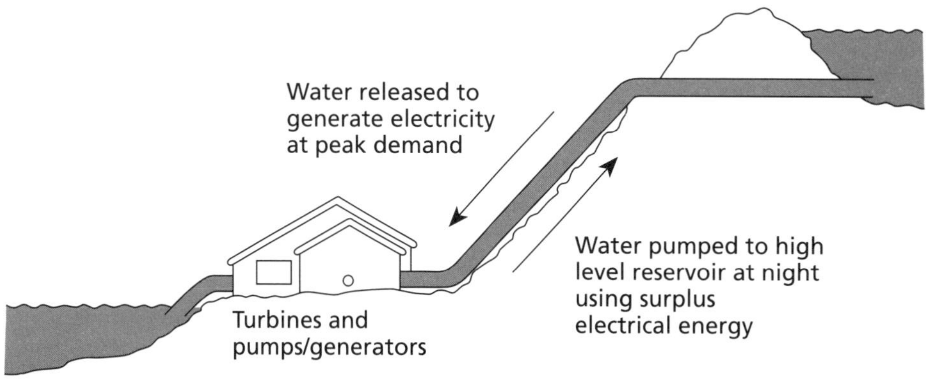

Letts Q&A

(i) Describe the energy transfer when the station is generating electricity.

....

....

.... (3)

(ii) In a pumped storage station, the maximum water flow downhill is 2.5×10^5 kg each second. This water falls through a height of 190 m. Calculate the energy lost by 2.5×10^5 kg of water in falling through a height of 190 m.

(3)

(iii) The energy from the water is transferred to electrical energy with an efficiency of 60%. Use the formula

$$\text{efficiency} = \frac{\text{useful power output}}{\text{total power input}}$$

to calculate the maximum power output of the station.

(3)

(iv) Suggest **one** factor that limits the efficiency of a pumped storage station when it is generating electricity.

....

....

.... (2)

(v) Pumped storage stations do not produce electricity. It takes more electrical energy to pump the water uphill than is recovered when it moves down. Suggest **two** advantages of using pumped storage rather than building more power stations to satisfy peak demand.

....

.... (2)

QUESTIONS

3 As an alternative to lifting a heavy load onto the back of a lorry, a ramp can be used to pull it up a slope.

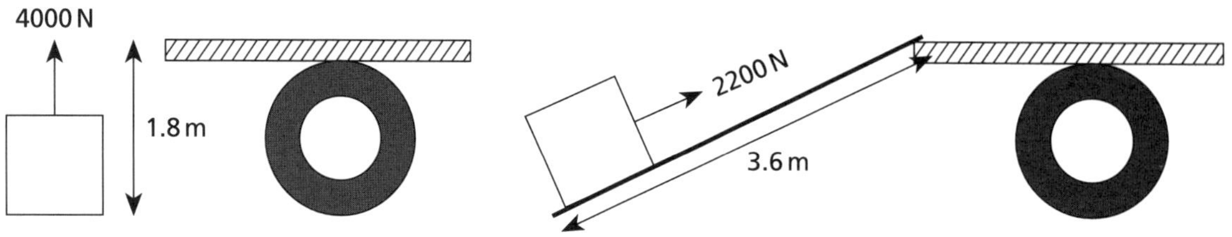

(a) Calculate the work done when the load is lifted onto the lorry.

(3)

(b) Calculate the work done by dragging the load up the ramp.

(2)

(c) The answer to (a) is the gain in gravitational potential energy of the load in each case. Explain why more work is needed to drag the load up the ramp than to lift it and suggest where the extra energy goes to.

....

....

.... (3)

(d) State **one** advantage of using the ramp instead of lifting the load.

.... (1)

4 The diagram shows a storage heater. The heating elements are turned on at night when electricity is cheap and heat is obtained from the concrete blocks during the day.

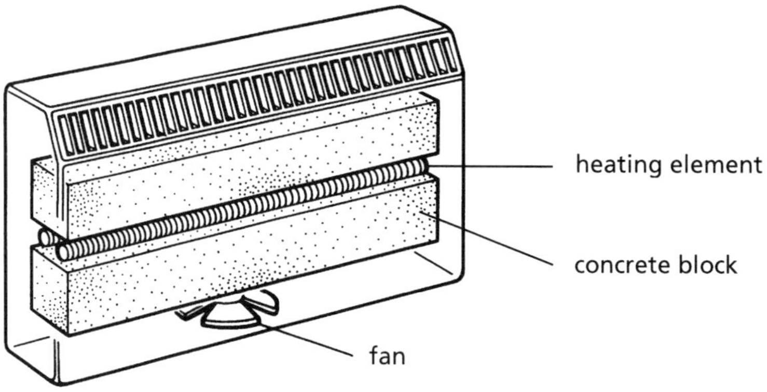

QUESTIONS

(a) The heater contains 85 kg of concrete which has a specific heat capacity of 1200 J/kg °C.

(i) How much energy is stored in the concrete when it is heated from 20 °C to 200 °C?

....

.... (3)

(ii) The elements have to supply more energy than the answer to (i).
Suggest a reason why.

.... (1)

(b) Describe as fully as you can the ways in which thermal energy is transferred from the concrete blocks to the room.

....

....

....

....

....

.... (6)

(c) The heater is used to maintain a constant room temperature of 20 °C.

(i) Describe what is happening to the energy being given out by the heater and explain why the room temperature is constant.

....

....

....

.... (4)

(ii) A householder wishes to make a house as 'energy-efficient' as possible. Explain whether it is possible for the energy from the heater to be recovered and re-used.

....

.... (2)

MEG 1994

Letts Q&A

11 Forces and their effects

REVISION SUMMARY

The **pressure** caused by a force is a measure of how effective it is at piercing or deforming the surface that it acts on. Drawing pins and scissors are designed so that the force exerts a large pressure and penetrates the surface. Skis and caterpillar tracks on vehicles ensure that the force is applied over a large area to reduce the pressure. The formula for calculating pressure is:

$$\text{pressure} = \frac{\text{force}}{\text{area}} \qquad \text{or in symbols} \qquad p = \frac{F}{A}$$

The unit of pressure is the pascal (Pa), which is equivalent to a N/m^2.

In hydraulic systems, liquids are used to transmit pressure. Because liquids exert an equal pressure in all directions, the pressure can be easily transmitted round corners. By changing the area over which the pressure acts, the force can be made bigger or smaller.

Taps, bicycle pedals and doors are common examples of forces being used to turn things round. How effective a force is at causing rotation depends not only on the size of the force, but also on the shortest distance from the line it acts along to the pivot. The **moment**, or turning effect, of a force is calculated using the formula:

$$\text{moment} = \text{force} \times \text{shortest (or perpendicular) distance from force line to pivot}$$

The moment, or turning effect, of a force is measured in N m. In situations where the turning effects of a number of forces cancel out, the object is balanced or in equilibrium. This is known as the 'law of moments' which states that:

> When an object is in **equilibrium**, the sum of the clockwise moments about any pivot is equal to the sum of the anticlockwise moments about that pivot.

Cars, bikes, buses, trains and other moving objects often have more than one force acting and so the overall effect of all the forces acting has to be taken into account. If the forces acting cancel out, there is no effect on the movement of the object; it either stays put or moves in a straight line at a constant speed. The average **speed** of a moving object is calculated using the equation:

$$\text{average speed} = \frac{\text{distance travelled}}{\text{time taken}} \qquad \text{or in symbols} \qquad v = \frac{s}{t}$$

When the forces are not balanced the effect is to change the speed or direction of an object. This is known as **acceleration**, which is calculated using the formula:

$$\text{acceleration} = \frac{\text{increase in velocity}}{\text{time taken}}$$

Acceleration can be thought of as the increase in speed per second and is measured in m/s^2 or $m\,s^{-2}$.

The acceleration caused by an unbalanced force depends on the mass being accelerated as well as the size of the unbalanced force – a double decker bus needs a much bigger force than a small car to give it the same acceleration. The equation which relates the mass of the object to the size of the unbalanced force and the acceleration it causes is:

$$\text{force} = \text{mass} \times \text{acceleration} \qquad \text{or in symbols} \qquad F = ma$$

Forces that cause movement are doing **work** and transferring **energy**. The amount of work done or energy transferred is calculated using the formula:

$$\text{work done} = \text{force} \times \text{distance moved in direction of force} \qquad \text{or in symbols} \qquad W = Fs$$

Work and energy are measured in joules (J).

REVISION SUMMARY

The rate at which work is done or energy is transferred is called the **power**; this is the work done by a force each second and is measured in watts (W). Power is calculated using the formula:

$$\text{power} = \frac{\text{work done or energy transferred}}{\text{time taken}} \quad \text{or in symbols} \quad P = \frac{W}{t}$$

Using a force to lift an object vertically is an example of transferring energy to gravitational potential energy (gpe for short). The gravitational potential energy gained by the object is calculated using the formula:

$$\text{change in gpe} = \text{weight} \times \text{change in height} \quad \text{or in symbols} \quad \text{gpe} = mg\Delta h$$

The symbol g stands for the gravitational field strength, which is the weight of each kg of material. The gravitational field strength at the surface of the Earth is about $10\,\text{N}\,\text{kg}^{-1}$ and that at the surface of the Moon is about $1.5\,\text{N}\,\text{kg}^{-1}$.

When an object is changing speed its kinetic energy (ke) is changing. The formula for kinetic energy is:

$$\text{kinetic energy} = {}^1/_2 \times \text{mass} \times (\text{speed})^2 \quad \text{or in symbols} \quad \text{ke} = {}^1/_2 mv^2$$

Moving objects also have **momentum**; momentum is a useful concept when predicting the outcome of a collision or using information about the outcome of a collision to deduce what happened before the collision occurred. The momentum of an object is calculated using the formula:

$$\text{momentum} = \text{mass} \times \text{velocity} \quad \text{or in symbols} \quad p = mv$$

Momentum is measured in N s or $\text{kg}\,\text{m}\,\text{s}^{-1}$ (the units are equivalent).

There are two important factors to remember about momentum; one is that the total amount of momentum of any system or group of objects stays the same and the second is that when adding the momentum of one object to that of another the direction has to be taken into account. The diagram illustrates this.

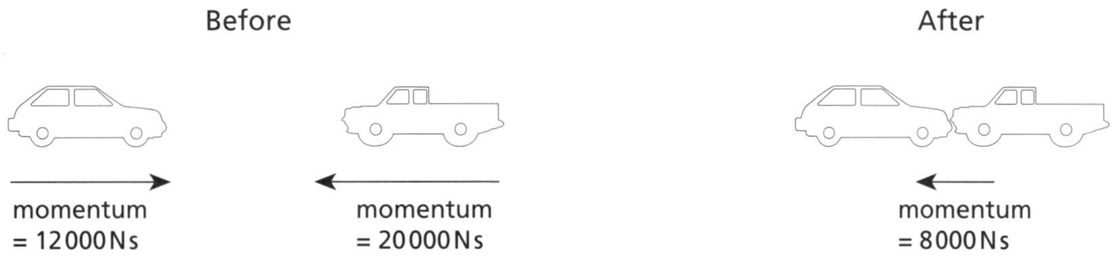

If you need to revise this subject more thoroughly, see the relevant topics in the Letts GCSE *Science Study Guide.*

QUESTIONS

1 The diagram shows a paper clip being held by a magnet.

(a) Draw two arrows to show the vertical forces on the paperclip and write a short description of each force.

....

.... (4)

(b) What can you tell about the relative size of the two forces? Give the reason for your answer.

....

.... (2)

(c) The paperclip is held between two identical magnets in the position shown in the diagram.

Describe and explain what will happen to the paperclip when it is released.

....

....

.... (3)

2 The pressure that a force causes is important in some winter sports.

(a) A skier who weighs 800 N is stood on two skis which each have an area of 0.4 m^2.

(i) Calculate the pressure on the snow.

(3)

(ii) State and explain the effect on the pressure when the skier lifts one leg (and ski) off the ground.

....

....

.... (3)

(b) Ice skaters cause enough pressure to melt the ice. A slim ice skater weighs only 500 N. The area of the blades on her skates is 2 cm^2 (0.0002 m^2). How much pressure is on the ice?

(2)

3 The turning effect of a force is used to pedal, steer and brake a bicycle. The diagrams show forces being used to push on a pedal which turns a crank.

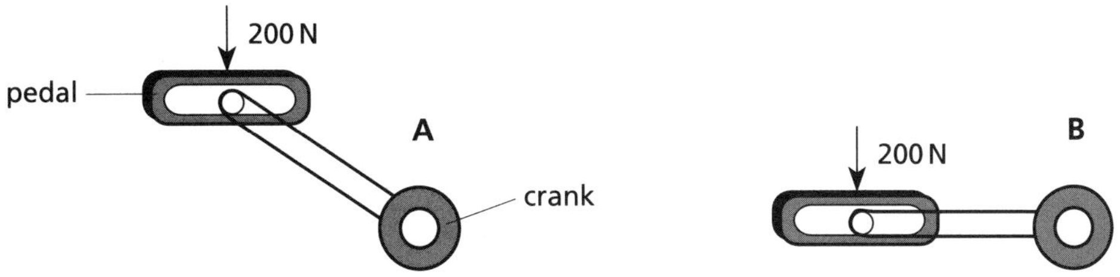

(a) Which force has the greater effect in turning the crank? Explain your answer fully.

....

....

.... (2)

(b) Calculate the moment of the force in diagram B if the distance from the force line to the pivot is 0.15 m.

....

....

....

.... (3)

QUESTIONS

(c) The diagram shows a cycle brake.

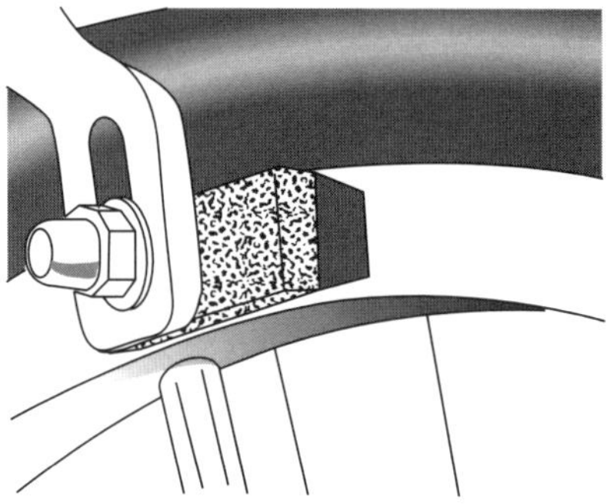

When the brakes are applied, a force of 120 N is applied at the rim of the wheel.

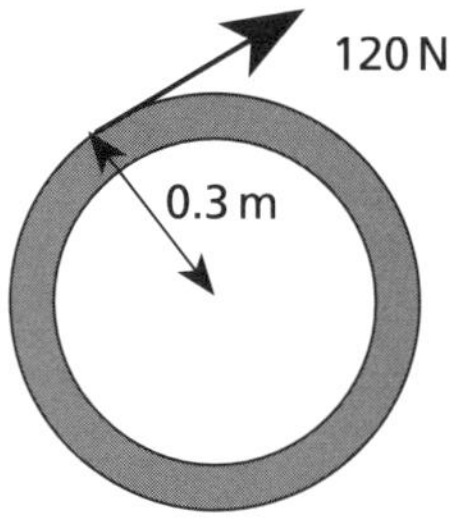

(i) Calculate the moment of this braking force.

(2)

(ii) Explain how you would expect the braking of a small-wheeled bicycle to compare with that of a large-wheeled one if the same braking force is applied to both bicycles.

....

....

.... (3)

(d) The graph shows how the speed of a cyclist changes on a short journey.

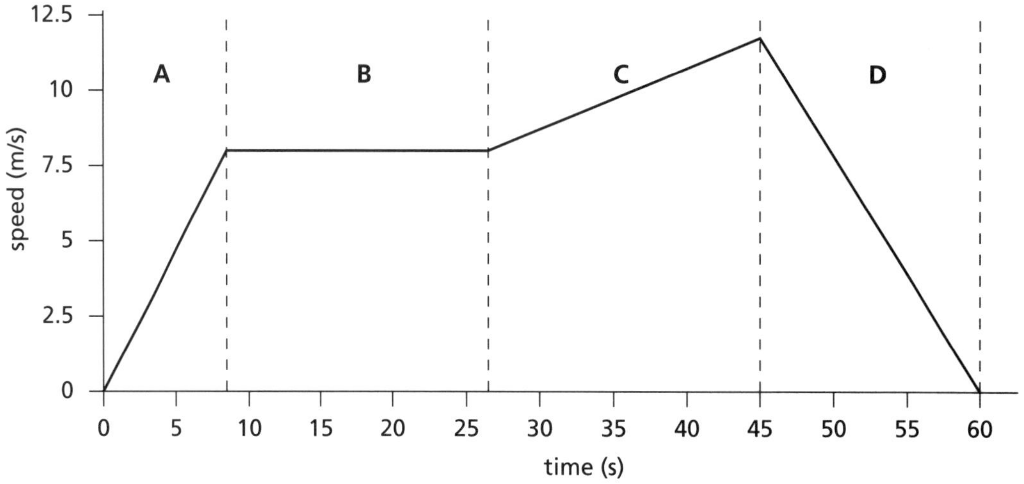

Letts Q&A

(i) Describe the motion of the cyclist in each of the sections shown on the graph.

A ....

B...

C ....

D .... (4)

(ii) Calculate the distance travelled by the cyclist in the period from 9 s to 26 s, section B on the graph.

(3)

(iii) Calculate the acceleration of the cyclist in the first 9 s, section A on the graph.

(3)

(iv) Calculate the unbalanced force needed to cause this acceleration if the combined mass of the cyclist and the cycle is 95 kg.

(3)

(v) Section A of the graph shows a constant acceleration. Suggest why it is likely in real life that the acceleration of the cyclist decreases as the speed increases.

....

.... (2)

(vi) The maximum speed of the cyclist during the journey shown on the graph is 12 m/s. Calculate the kinetic energy of the cycle and cyclist at this speed.

(3)

QUESTIONS

(vii) Calculate the braking force required to stop the cycle and cyclist in section D of the graph.

(4)

(viii) Calculate the braking distance in section D of the graph. (*Hint: the* ***average*** *speed is not 12 m/s.*)

(3)

(ix) Assuming the same braking force is used, calculate the braking distance from a speed of 6 m/s.

(3)

(x) Explain why the braking distance from a speed of 12 m/s is four times that from a speed of 6 m/s.

....

....

.... (3)

4 (a) How can the momentum of an object be calculated?

....

.... (2)

(b) In a collision momentum is always conserved. What does this mean?

....

.... (2)

(c) Two trolleys are placed on a frictionless runway as shown in the diagram below. Trolley **A** has a protruding pin, and trolley **B** is fitted with a piece of soft cork so that the trolleys will stick together after colliding.

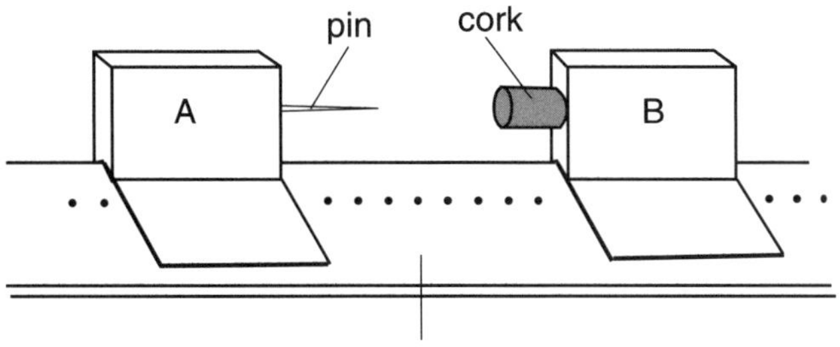

Trolley **A** has a mass of 2 kg, and trolley **B** has a mass of 1 kg. Trolley **B** is stationary. Trolley **A** strikes trolley **B** at a speed of 6 m/s. Both trolleys then move to the right together.

(i) Calculate the speed at which trolleys A and B jointly move after the collision.

....

....

....

.... (4)

(ii) Calculate the change in kinetic energy which occurs during the collision.

....

....

....

.... (4)

NEAB 1995

12 Light and sound

REVISION SUMMARY

Sound is carried to our ears by a to-and-fro movement of air molecules. This to-and-fro movement starts with a vibrating object, such as a loudspeaker, which sets the air molecules into a **longitudinal wave** motion where the vibrations are along the direction in which the wave is travelling.

The maximum amount of displacement (movement to one side or the other) of the air molecules is called the **amplitude** of the wave; the greater the amplitude, the louder the sound. The graph shows how the movement of an individual air molecule changes with time.

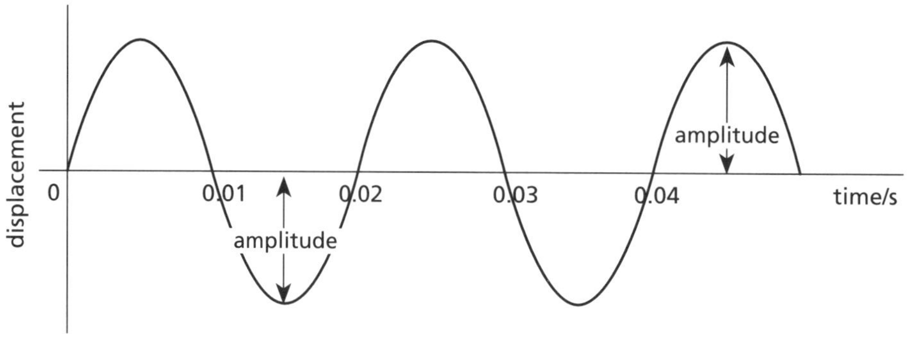

As well as showing the amplitude, the time scale on the graph enables the **frequency** to be measured. The frequency of a wave is the number of oscillations per second. The sound wave shown on the graph does one complete oscillation in 0.02 or 1/50 second so it has a frequency of 50 waves per second, or 50 hertz (Hz). The frequency of a sound wave determines its pitch; 50 Hz is quite a low-pitched sound, while frequencies of 1000 Hz or more are high-pitched.

Measurements of the **wavelength** (the distance occupied by one complete cycle of the wave) and frequency allow the speed of sound to be calculated using the formula:

$$\text{speed} = \text{frequency} \times \text{wavelength} \quad \text{or in symbols} \quad v = f\lambda$$

Resonance is the name given to the build-up of large-amplitude vibrations when an object is forced to vibrate at a frequency which is equal to its natural frequency of vibration. Pushing a child on a swing is an example of resonance – the amplitude of the swing's vibration increases when the frequency of pushing coincides with the natural frequency of the swing, so that it receives a push once every complete oscillation. Resonance can be a nuisance when it leads to unwanted vibration, such as in a washing machine or spin-drier. Electrical resonance is used to select which of the signals being received by the aerial a television or radio is tuned to.

Light is a small part of a family of waves called the **electromagnetic spectrum**. Most objects do not give off light, so we rely on reflected light to be able to see them. All but the smoothest of surfaces reflect light in all directions. Mirrors are smooth surfaces that reflect light in a predictable way – the angles of incidence and reflection are equal. The reflection of light by a mirror causes a virtual image to be formed. Our eye–brain system assumes that light travels in straight lines, so when we look into a mirror the reflected light looks to have come from a point the same distance behind the mirror as the object is in front of it.

Mirrors are not the only things that can cause the direction in which light travels to change; light can also change direction when it passes through transparent objects such as glass. The change in speed when light passes from one substance to another is called **refraction**. This causes a change in wavelength and, except when light hits the boundary at a right angle, a change in direction. Although the wavelength and speed both change when light is refracted, the frequency, which determines the colour of the light, remains constant.

Light does not always pass into the new substance when it meets a boundary. Light travelling from glass to air is totally internally reflected for angles of incidence greater than 42°. Total internal reflection is used in bicycle reflectors, prism binoculars, Cat's-eyes and fibre optics.

The table shows the main parts of the electromagnetic spectrum and their uses.

Wave	gamma rays	X-rays	ultraviolet	visible light	infrared	microwaves	radio waves
Typical wavelength (m)	1×10^{-12}	1×10^{-9}	1×10^{-7}	5×10^{-7}	1×10^{-6}	1×10^{-1}	100
Use	sterilizing medical equipment	X-ray photographs	treatment of skin disorders; responsible for suntans	seeing; transmitting data	heating; armchair operation of TV equipment	cooking; transmitting data	broadcasting

The shorter wavelength waves are the most penetrative and also the most ionizing, so they pose the greatest dangers. Exposure to waves of shorter wavelength than light should be limited.

All electromagnetic waves are **transverse waves** – the vibrations are at right angles to the direction of travel. Radio waves from an aerial are **polarized**, which means that the vibrations are only in one plane. Light waves from a light source such as a lamp or the Sun are unpolarized. Light can be polarized by passing it through materials such as the Polaroid used in some sunglasses. Light is partially polarized when it is reflected.

All waves spread out when they pass through a narrow opening; this is called **diffraction**. The amount of spreading depends on the size of the opening relative to the wavelength; if the opening is hundreds of wavelengths wide then very little spreading occurs, with maximum spreading when the opening is equal to the wavelength. Sound waves (typical wavelength 1 m) spread out when passing through a doorway, but light waves do not.

When two or more waves cross at any point they interfere with each other. When waves interfere they can combine to give an increase or decrease in disturbance at that point. When two wave crests or troughs combine constructive interference takes place; a wave crest and a trough combine to interfere destructively.

Interference can be seen in surface water waves using a ripple tank; two dippers vibrating in step produce lines of constructive and destructive interference. The separation of the lines of interference increases with increasing wavelength and distance from the sources but decreases when the sources are placed further apart. The interference of sound waves can be heard if two loudspeakers driven from the same signal generator are used as wave sources. Interference of light waves is more difficult to arrange using two sources, but can be readily observed using a diffraction grating.

If you need to revise this subject more thoroughly, see the relevant topics in the Letts GCSE *Science Study Guide*.

QUESTIONS

1 (a) A tuning fork is designed to produce a note of one particular frequency. The one shown in the diagram produces 'middle C', which has a frequency of 256 Hz.

(i) Describe how the tuning fork produces the note 'middle C'.

....

....

....

.... (2)

(ii) A tuning fork with shorter prongs produces a note of frequency 512 Hz. In what way does this note sound different to the 256 Hz note ?

.... (1)

(iii) The speed of sound in air is 330 m/s. Calculate the wavelength of a sound wave of frequency 256 Hz.

(3)

(b) The diagram represents a sound wave travelling in air.

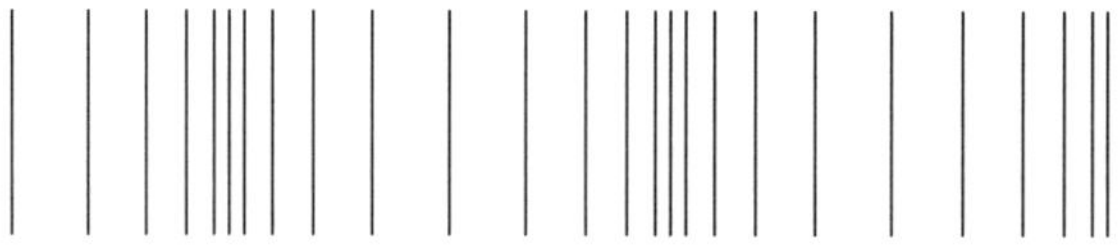

(i) Mark on the diagram a distance that represents one wavelength of the wave. (1)

(ii) Describe the movement of the air molecules as the wave passes from left to right.

....

.... (2)

(iii) Describe how the movement of the air molecules changes when the loudness of the sound is increased.

....

.... (2)

QUESTIONS

(c) Sounds do not last for very long. When a sound is made in a room the energy is quickly absorbed by the objects that it hits, forcing them to vibrate as it does so.
The vibrations are usually of small amplitude and are not noticed. Sometimes sound waves can cause a particular object to vibrate with a large amplitude. Explain how this can occur.

....

....

.... (3)

2 (a) Mirrors and flat surfaces of water or glass reflect light in a predictable way. A person standing by a lake can see a tree on the opposite side of the lake and also an image of the tree in the lake.

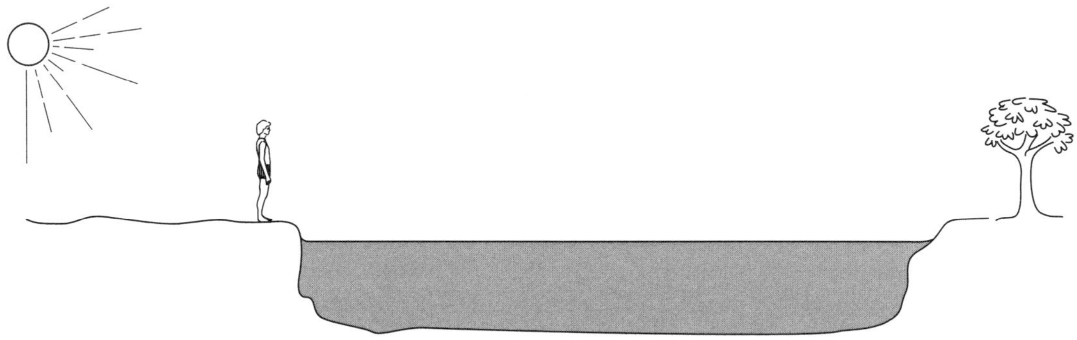

(i) Explain how light from the Sun enables the person to see the tree.

.... (1)

(ii) Draw on the diagram to show how light from the tree can be reflected by the lake to the person's eye.

.... (1)

(iii) Sketch on the diagram the image of the tree that the person sees. (3)

(iv) Is the image a real or a virtual one? Explain how you can tell.

....

.... (2)

(b) Not all of the light is reflected at the water surface; some passes into the water, where it slows down. The diagram on the next page represents wavefronts of light approaching the water surface from two directions.

QUESTIONS

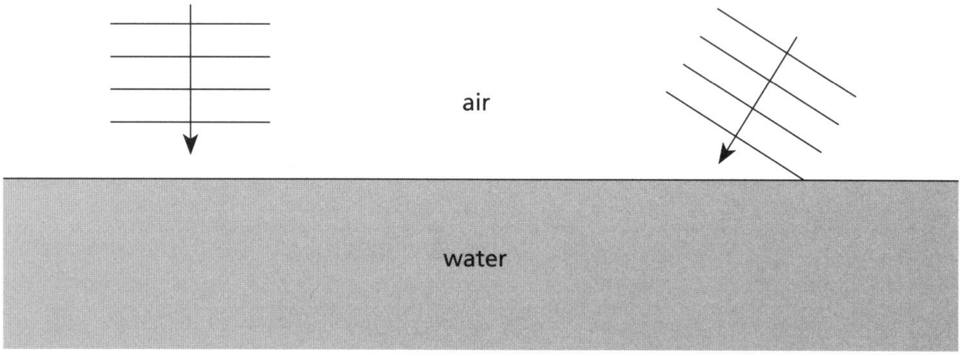

The speed of light in water is approximately three-quarters of its speed in air. Complete the diagrams to show the wavefronts as they pass through the water. (4)

(c) When light strikes a water surface both the reflected light and the refracted light become partially plane-polarized. The reflected light is horizontally polarized and the refracted light is vertically polarized. Draw diagrams to show the difference between horizontal and vertical polarization of light.

(3)

(d) Suggest how the Polaroid material in some sunglasses is able to reduce the 'glare' caused by the reflection of light from a water surface. A diagram could help to make your answer clear.

(3)

3 Radio and television aerials are designed to absorb energy from waves of a particular wavelength and frequency. VHF radio aerials are designed to receive waves with a frequency of approximately 1×10^8 Hz.

(a) The speed of radio waves in air is 3.0×10^8 m/s. Calculate the wavelength of a radio wave with a frequency of 1.0×10^8 Hz.

(3)

(b) When an aerial absorbs energy from radio waves an electrical oscillation is set up within the aerial. Radio waves of frequency 1×10^8 Hz cause an oscillation which resonates. Suggest why an oscillation at this frequency resonates but one at a frequency of 1.0×10^6 Hz does not.

QUESTIONS

....

....

.... (3)

(c) Radar uses short wavelength radio waves emitted in a narrow beam. The diagram shows how this is achieved by reflecting the beam from a convex and then a concave reflector.

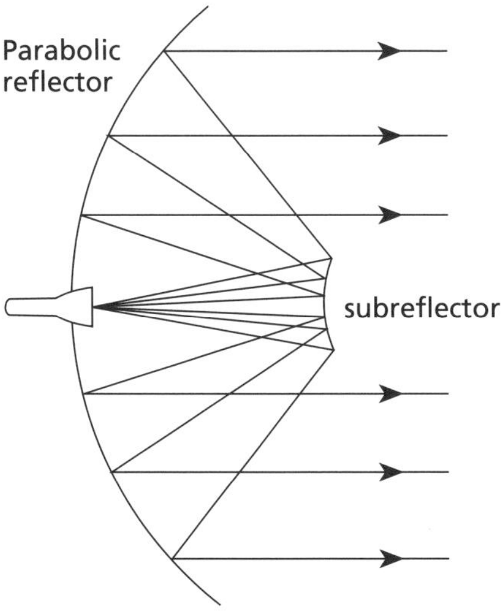

The larger the diameter of the reflector used, the less the beam spreads out.

(i) Suggest why narrow beams of radiation are used for radar.

....

.... (1)

(ii) Explain why a large diameter reflector has to be used to reduce the beam spread.

....

....

.... (2)

(iii) Draw a diagram to show what you would expect to happen if the diameter of the reflector used was equal to the wavelength of the radio waves.

(2)

13 The Earth's place in the universe

REVISION SUMMARY

The **universe** is thought to have begun in an enormous explosion about 15 billion years ago. The name 'universe' means everything: stars, planets, asteroids, galaxies and everything that exists.

Within the universe there are groups of stars called **galaxies**. Our star is the Sun and our galaxy is the Milky Way, which is a whirling spiral, held together by the attractive gravitational forces that act between massive objects.

Gravitational forces act between all objects that have mass, but they are only significant when one of the objects is very massive. There is, for example, a gravitational force between two pencils placed one centimetre apart on a desktop, but it is a tiny force and is not big enough to overcome the frictional forces that resist motion.

Gravitational attraction between the planets and the Sun keep the planets in orbit around the Sun. The orbits are actually ellipses, but they are almost circular.

All circular motion requires an unbalanced force acting towards the centre of the circle. Without the gravitational pull, the planets would not stay in orbit around the Sun. Imagine whirling a rubber bung tied to a piece of string; you have to keep pulling on the string to keep the bung going round in a circle.

Gravitational forces act between objects, with each object pulling the other. While the Earth's pull on the Moon keeps the Moon in orbit around the Earth, the most obvious effect of the Moon's pull on the Earth is in causing the movement of water that creates tides.

Although the Earth has only one natural satellite, there are many artificial ones. Like the Moon, they are kept in orbit by the gravitational attraction of the Earth. This gravitational attraction decreases with increasing distance from the Earth. Low orbit satellites go round the Earth in one and a half hours, but communications satellites are placed further from the Earth where the orbit time is twenty-four hours; in this way they stay above the same point on the Earth's surface.

The Sun is the energy source for the Earth and the rest of the solar system. This energy comes from the fusion reaction taking place in the Sun. Our Sun, like the other stars in the universe, probably started life as a cloud of hydrogen. Gravitational forces caused the cloud to contract and become hot, reaching a temperature of millions of degrees. At these temperatures hydrogen nuclei join together to form helium nuclei, a reaction which releases a large amount of energy.

Our Sun is not as old as the universe. The solar system is thought to have been formed from material ejected by an exploding star. The core of this cloud of material formed the Sun, with the outermost material condensing to form the planets. In addition to the nine planets, there is the asteroid belt and, on the far reaches of the solar system, collections of ice and dust known as comets. The comets have very long orbit times, often hundreds of years.

The inner planets, Mercury, Venus, Earth and Mars, are the denser ones in the solar system; they have a high concentration of metals. Jupiter and Saturn are composed largely of hydrogen and helium. Jupiter has many moons, one of which, Io, is the most geologically active body in the solar system. Little is known about the composition of the three outermost planets. Uranus and Neptune are thought to be composed mainly of hydrogen and helium, but Pluto is thought to consist mainly of ice and rock.

The universe is still expanding, as it has been doing since its formation. When the paths of the galaxies are plotted, all these paths trace back to the same point. This is thought to be the point where the universe was created. The age of the universe is estimated by measuring the speed at which the galaxies are moving away from each other and extrapolating back to the beginning of time.

There are three possibilities for the future of the universe. It may carry on expanding for ever, or the gravitational forces may slow down the expansion and eventually cause it to contract again with catastrophic results. The third model is that the gravitational forces are not strong enough to cause a collapse but are just strong enough to prevent continued expansion, so the universe will eventually reach a stable size.

If you need to revise this subject more thoroughly, see the relevant topics in the *Letts GCSE Science Study Guide*.

QUESTIONS

1 The diagram represents the motion of the two innermost planets, Mercury (M) and Venus (V).

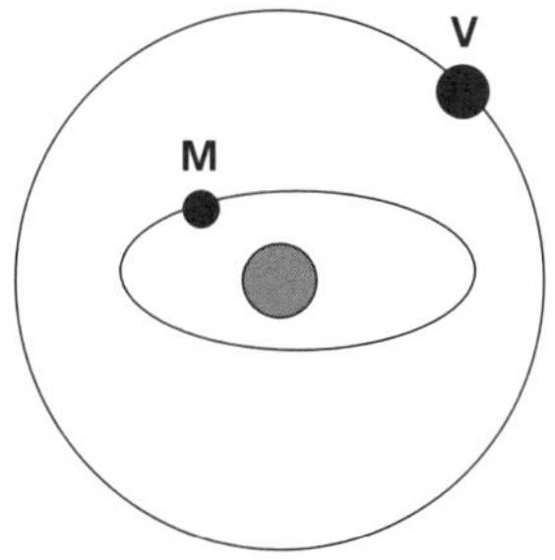

The table gives some data about these planets.

	Mercury	Venus
Mass (kg)	3.3×10^{23}	4.9×10^{24}
Radius (m)	2.4×10^{6}	6.1×10^{6}
Density (g/cm^3)	5.4	5.3
Orbital period (Earth days)	88	224
Distance from Sun compared to Earth	0.39	0.72
Mean orbital speed (km/s)	48	35
Atmosphere	none	carbon dioxide with sulphuric acid clouds

Use the diagram and the information in the table to answer the questions that follow.

(a) The speed of Venus in its orbit around the Sun hardly changes, but that of Mercury varies considerably. Suggest why this is.

....

.... (2)

(b) Describe and explain how you would expect the speed of Mercury to change as it orbits the Sun.

....

....

.... (4)

(c) Suggest **two** reasons why the time taken to complete one orbit of the Sun is longer for Venus than for Mercury.

....

.... (2)

QUESTIONS

(d) Venus is similar in size and mass to the Earth. What does this information tell you about the densities of the three innermost planets?

.... (1)

(e) Mercury and the Earth's Moon both show evidence of many collisions with meteors. These are thought to have occurred in the early part of the solar system's lifetime. Suggest **three** reasons why there is little evidence of collisions on Earth and Venus.

....

....

.... (3)

(f) Space probes that have landed on Venus to photograph the surface have had a very short operational life. Suggest **two** reasons for this.

....

.... (2)

2 The universe is thought to have started with an enormous explosion. The first substances that formed after the explosion were hydrogen and helium. Heavier elements were later formed in stars.

(a) Suggest how the heavier elements could have formed.

....

.... (2)

(b) Explain why our solar system could not have been formed at the same time as the first stars in the universe.

....

.... (2)

(c) One theory about the origin of the solar system is that it was formed from a spinning cloud of dust that was part of the remains of an exploding supernova. Explain how this theory explains the fact that the innermost planets are denser than the outer planets.

....

.... (2)

(d) The universe is still expanding, but the rate of expansion is decreasing. Suggest why the rate of expansion is decreasing.

QUESTIONS

....

.... (2)

(e) Explain how the expansion of the universe supports the theory that it started as a single explosion.

....

.... (2)

3 The Earth has many satellites. One of these, the Moon, is the Earth's natural satellite. The Earth and the Moon exert forces on each other.

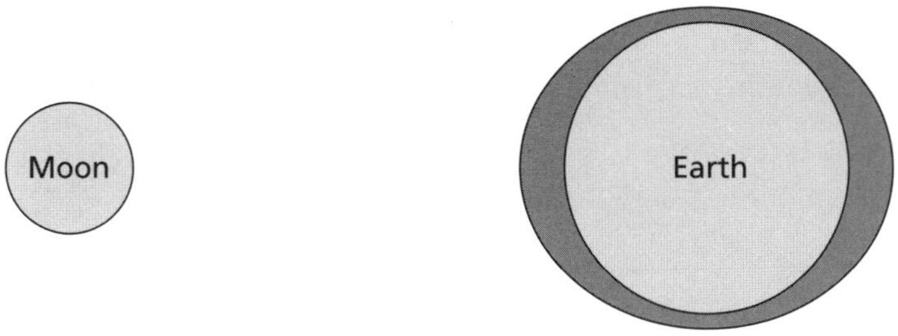

(a) Draw an arrow on the diagram to show the force of the Earth on the Moon. (1)

(b) Explain why the water covering the Earth's surface is deeper on the sides facing and opposite to the Moon.

....

.... (2)

(c) Use the diagram to explain how tides are formed.

....

....

.... (3)

(d) Radioactivity measurements on rock samples from the Moon indicate that the Moon is approximately the same age as the solar system. It is not known where the Moon came from. What evidence should astronomers look for in Moon rock that could give clues as to the Moon's origin?

....

.... (2)

Answers

1 LIFE PROCESSES

Question	Answer	Mark

Examiner's tip This question is about parts of the body and the jobs they do. It is a very common question, especially on Central tier papers.

Question	Answer	Mark
1	A is the large intestine/colon	1
	It absorbs water from the waste material	1
	B is a kidney	1
	It removes waste materials such as urea and water from the blood	1
	C is the liver	1
	The liver has several jobs. Any one of the following answers would be acceptable.	
	You should have named one from: adjusts the level of glucose in the blood, makes bile, stores iron, removes old red blood cells, produces heat, stores vitamins and minerals, removes nitrogen	1
	D is the heart	1
	It pumps blood round the body	1
	E is a lung	1
	It exchanges oxygen for carbon dioxide	1

Examiner's tip You do not get a mark for saying that the lung is for breathing. Breathing is the movement of the diaphragm and the intercostal muscles which cause air to move in and out of the lungs. The important job is gas exchange.

Question	Answer	Mark
	F is the stomach	1
	It digests food/contains the food whilst being digested	1
	G is the bladder	1
	It stores liquid waste (urine)	1

Question	Answer	Mark
2 (a)	Any one from: Leaves are broad Leaves are flat Leaves have a large surface area	1

Examiner's tip These are all ways leaves have adapted. You will not be given marks for saying, for example, 'the cuticle is transparent', which is a piece of information given in (b) and not an adaptation.

Question	Answer	Mark
(b) (i)	This allows light through to the palisade layer	1
(ii)	This part of the leaf receives most light	1
(iii)	The air spaces allow oxygen and carbon dioxide to diffuse to and from the cells	1

Examiner's tip The air spaces are also close to the stomata where gases enter and leave the leaf. This would be an acceptable alternative answer.

Question		Answer	Mark
(c)		Chlorophyll	1
(d)	(i)	More light increases the rate of photosynthesis	1
	(ii)	Lowering the temperature decreases the rate of photosynthesis	1

Examiner's tip Here the question is about the rate of photosynthesis. Your answer should be in terms of increasing and decreasing the rate of photosynthesis. Weaker candidates answer in terms of the growth of the plant, e.g. the plant grows better. This vagueness is not acceptable and would receive no credit.

Question		Answer	Mark
(e)		carbon dioxide + water $\rightarrow$ carbohydrates + oxygen	1

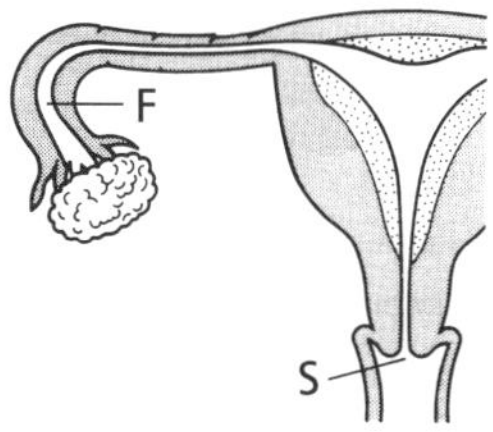

Question		Answer	Mark
3 (a)	(i)	Fertilization (F) takes place in the fallopian tube, the tube that links the ovary to the uterus	1
		The sperm are released (S) at the top of the vagina	1
	(ii)	The sperm has a tail	1
		The tail propels the sperm	1
(b)	(i)	The amniotic fluid protects the embryo from injury/acts as a shock absorber It keeps the embryo moist It keeps it at a constant temperature	2

Examiner's tip There are three points here. You get 1 mark for each of the first two points made.

Question		Answer	Mark
	(ii)	Oxygenated blood from the placenta travels down the umbilical cord	1
		The deoxygenated blood from the embryo returns to the placenta through the umbilical cord	1
		Gas exchange takes place in the placenta by diffusion	1

Examiner's tip It is important to appreciate that the mother's blood and the embryo's blood do not mix. Both travel through the placenta; gases and other substances are exchanged by diffusion. Your answer should make this clear and you should include the word diffusion in your answer. There are 3 marks for this part and it is reasonable to expect to have to make three points.

Question		Answer	Mark
4 (a)		The rate of metabolism increases	1
		This releases energy	1
(b)		Heat is produced during exercise	1
		This has to be lost to keep the body temperature constant	1
(c)		Glucose from the blood is changed into glycogen	1
		This is stored in the liver and muscles	1
(d)	(i)	The glucose level rises several times a day	1
		The hormone level needs to increase at these times to remove the glucose	1

Examiner's tip Answering this part of the question requires you to interpret the graph correctly.

Question			Answer	Mark
		(ii)	Glucose is used in exercise	1
			So less hormone is needed as there is less glucose to be removed from the blood	1

2 INHERITANCE AND EVOLUTION

Question			Answer	Mark
1	(a)	(i)	Accidental loss of an arm	1
		(ii)	*Either* blood group *or* eye colour *or* gender/sex	1
		(iii)	Mass	1
	(b)		*Either* genes *or* chromosomes *or* DNA	1
2	(a)		Father = xy	1
			Eggs = x x Sperms = x y	1
			Daughter = xx Son = xy	1

Examiner's tip This diagram shows how the sex of a child is determined by the chromosomes it inherits from its father.

Question			Answer	Mark
	(b)		**G** 1 in 2 or 50% **H** zero	1
			The gene for the disease must be dominant	1
			Because two of the offspring of A and B show the symptoms, but only one parent has the disease	1
			Children inherit one chromosome from each pair in each parent	1
			So there is a 50:50 chance that the offspring of C and D will inherit the gene from their father	1
			Neither E nor F has the disease, so they cannot have the gene, therefore H cannot inherit it	1

Examiner's tip In this type of question there are more marks for explaining how you arrive at your answer than for the answer itself. Before writing your final answer, it is a good idea to jot down the main points you want to make and then put them in a logical order.

Question			Answer	Mark
3	(a)		The farmers could have chosen the cows with a high milk yield	1
			And only bred from these cows	1
			This process would be repeated through several generations	1

Question	Answer	Mark

Examiner's tip This is an example of selective breeding. Candidates sometimes get confused between selective breeding (which occurs on Higher and Central tier papers) and genetic engineering (which only occurs on Higher tier papers). Genetic engineering requires genetic changes within the DNA.

(b)	Fewer cows are needed to produce the milk	1
	This uses less land/less food	1

Examiner's tip Here weaker candidates will gives answers such as 'save money'. There is an economic answer, but it has to be expressed clearly. For example, the same amount of milk can be produced from feeding fewer cows. This is worth 2 marks.

4	The correct diagram is on page 8. Your diagram should show:	
	Each chromosome makes an exact copy of itself	1
	These copies then separate	1
	One set of chromosomes forms at each end of the cell	1
	The cell then divides into two, each of which is an exact copy of the original cell	1

Examiner's tip The processes of mitosis and meiosis are very important. Make sure you have clearly understood these two processes. Meiosis occurs during reproduction. Mitosis occurs when cells replicate.

---

5 (a)	A gene mutation occurred	1
	This could have been caused by a miscopy or radiation damage	1
(b)	The dark-coloured moths are camouflaged	1
	More have survived and reproduced	1

---

6 (a)	Your diagram should show that A always pairs with T	1
	and C pairs with G	1

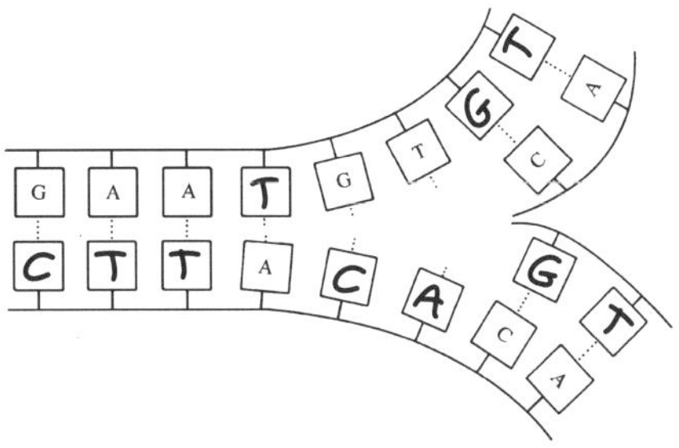

(b)	The DNA determines the characteristics of the individual	1
	All the cells in the body should have the same genetic information	1
(c) (i)	Isoleucine, Glycine, Cysteine (must be in this order)	1

Question			Answer	Mark
		(ii)	CGAGAAGTA	1
	(d)	(i)	A mutation	1
		(ii)	Any inherited disease such as cystic fibrosis, sickle-cell anaemia or haemophilia	1
		(iii)	Mutations cause variation, i.e. individuals with different characteristics	1
			These new characteristics can be beneficial and help an organism to survive in its environment or enable it to survive in a new environment	1

Examiner's tip Questions involving DNA replication are common on Higher tier GCSE Science papers.

3 POPULATIONS AND HUMAN INFLUENCES

Question			Answer	Mark
1	(a)	(i)	The algae is the producer	1
		(ii)	The small molluscs are the primary consumers	1
		(iii)	There would be a lot more molluscs than ospreys	1
	(b)	(i)	The number of ospreys was falling; this could have been caused by a decrease in their food supply	1
		(ii)	1969 to 1970	1

Examiner's tip This is the minimum point on the graph. After DDT stopped being used the population of ospreys increased.

		(iii)	The osprey takes in the DDT that was contained in a large quantity of algae	1

Examiner's tip The idea of toxic substances being concentrated in higher members of a food chain is very common on GCSE Science papers.

2	(a)	(i)	It decreases and then increases	1
		(ii)	There are microorganisms in the waste	1
			Which use up oxygen during respiration	1

Examiner's tip You could use the scientific terms bacteria or saprophytes to describe the microorganisms in the waste, but terms such as 'germs' or 'bugs' would not gain credit.

		(iii)	The fish would suffocate through lack of oxygen	1
			Some will die *or* numbers will decrease	1
		(iv)	It is high	1

Question	Answer	Mark

Examiner's tip You are not expected to know anything about mayfly nymphs to answer this question, but you are expected to interpret the data in the graph.

(b)	(i)	[A] The young trout have less blackfly larvae to eat	1
		So they will eat more mayfly nymphs	1
		[B] There are more one-celled algae	1
		So mayfly nymphs have more food	1

Examiner's tip An equally valid answer is that there are more filamentous algae, so more midge larvae for the trout to eat, hence they eat fewer mayfly nymphs. This would get both marks.

	(ii)	The algae absorb energy from the Sun in photosynthesis	1
		Energy is lost at each link of a food chain	1
		There are fewer links in the young trouts' food chain	1
		So they receive a higher proportion of the Sun's energy	1

Examiner's tip The last two points could have been gained by stating that there are more links in the mature trouts' food chain so they will receive proportionally less of the Sun's energy.

(c)		Be less than at C	1
		The water is warmer at H	1
		So the oxygen concentration will decrease	1
		This will cause the suffocation of some fish	1

Examiner's tip The fish population at H would decrease to a level that could be supported by the reduced oxygen concentration.

4 ECOLOGY

Question			Answer	Mark
1	(a)	(i)	Gardener A	1
		(ii)	The rotting occurs faster at a higher temperature	1
	(b)		This brings the undecomposed material into the warmer centre of the heap	1
	(c)		The rotting will slow down because more heat will be lost from the heap	1

Question			Answer	Mark
2	(a)	(i)	C	1

Examiner's tip The question tells you that there is one oak tree. The oak tree bar must be short (either B or C). There are more caterpillars than owls, and so C is the correct answer. Many candidates wrongly assume that A or B is correct. They seem to have more regularity.

		(ii)	Biomass is the total mass of living animals and plants	1
		(iii)	The pyramid should look like this:	2

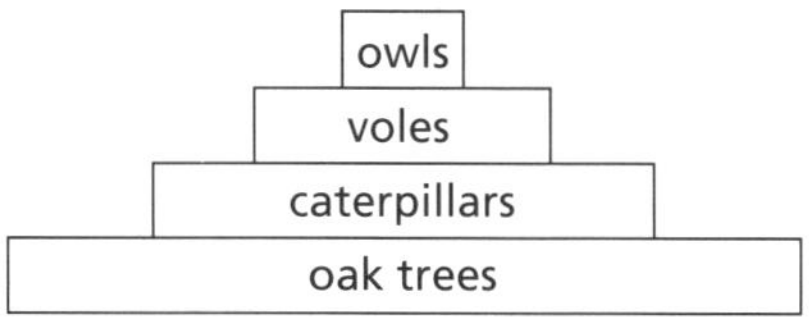

		(iv)	Energy is lost by egestion *or* excretion *or* heat *or* abscission (loss of leaves, flowers, branches)	1
	(b)		The woodland community will become smaller	1
			Because there is less of its habitat available	1

Examiner's tip Again do not forget to explain the effect. An alternative answer might be given in terms of increased pollution.

3	(a)		Plants obtain energy from the Sun	1
	(b)		The rabbit does not eat all of the plant	1
			The rabbit does not absorb all the energy in the food it eats	1
	(c)	(i)	Excretion/movement/heat to keep warm	1
		(ii)	40	1
	(d)	(i)	B	1
		(ii)	The average mass of the rabbits	1
			The number of rabbits per acre or hectare	1
	(e)		**Advantages:**	
			Shooting: all the land is available for agriculture	1
			Natural predators: these need a constant food supply and will always be hunting	1
			Disadvantages:	
			Shooting: unreliable; the noise of the gun scares the rabbits back into their burrows	1
			Natural predators: they could be a danger to other farm animals	1

5 THE PROPERTIES, CLASSIFICATION AND STRUCTURE OF MATERIALS

Question			Answer	Mark
1	(a)	(i)	The electron arrangement in a sodium atom is 2,8,1. When a sodium ion is produced, the outer electron is lost. The electron arrangement of a sodium ion is 2,8	1

Question	Answer	Mark
(ii)	The electron arrangement of a chlorine atom is 2,8,7. When a chloride ion is formed the atom gains an electron and so has an electron arrangement of 2,8,8	1

Examiner's tip You should use the Periodic Table to work out the electron arrangement of each atom. Sodium has an atomic number of 11 and so a sodium atom contains 11 electrons. The first shell holds a maximum of 2 electrons, the second shell 8 electrons. The remaining electron enters the third shell. Similarly, chlorine has an atomic number of 17 and therefore contains 17 electrons. The third shell contains 7 electrons. Now, to get the correct answers you need to know that a sodium atom loses an electron and a chlorine atom gains an electron.

Question	Answer	Mark
(iii)	Ionic bonding	1
(b) (i)	The diagram shows a small part of a sodium chloride crystal. If this is extended in all directions the cubic shape will produce a cube-shaped crystal	1
(ii)	Melting sodium chloride requires the breaking of all of the bonds between sodium and chloride ions	1
	These are very strong electrostatic bonds and a high temperature/lots of energy is required to break them	1
(iii)	Electricity is carried by free electrons or free ions	1
	There are no free electrons and the ions are held rigidly in the lattice, unable to move	1
(iv)	Melting will break down the lattice and produce free ions	1
	Sodium ions move towards the cathode and chloride ions towards the anode	1
2 (a)	As the distance from the nose increases, the surface temperature decreases	1
(b)	40 m	1

Examiner's tip This question does not require previous knowledge. You must interpret the information in the graph.

Question	Answer	Mark
3 (a) (i)	Potassium has an atomic number of 19	1
	Atom contains 19 protons and 19 electrons	1
	Contains (39 − 19), i.e. 20, neutrons	1
	Electron arrangement is 2,8,8,1	1
	Protons and neutrons in the nucleus	1
		(Any four points to be awarded)

Examiner's tip It is probably best to draw an annotated diagram to help answer this question. This diagram would receive 4 marks without any other words.

Question **Answer** **Mark**

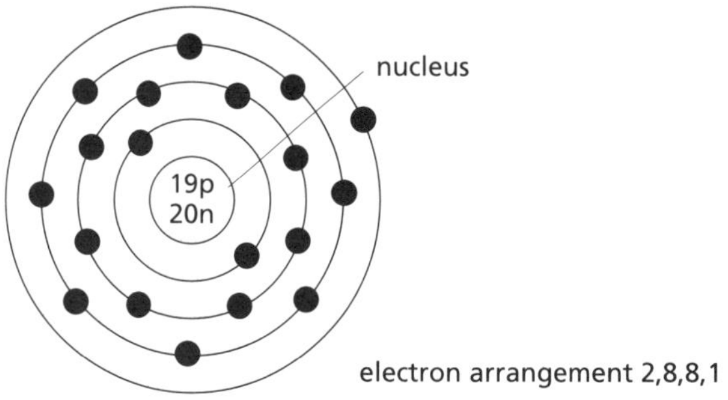

(ii) Calcium contains one more proton than potassium **1**
Calcium nucleus holds on to outer electrons better, making it less reactive **1**

Examiner's tip Potassium and calcium are adjacent in the Periodic Table. A calcium atom is also slightly smaller than a potassium atom which also helps.

(iii) Non-metals react by gaining electrons to form negative ions **1**
Bromine contains one more proton and therefore attracts electrons better **1**

(b) Barium reacts steadily with cold water **1**
To produce hydrogen and barium hydroxide **1**

Examiner's tip Selenium and bromine are adjacent in the Periodic Table. Barium is similar in reactivity to an alkali metal. There is an increase in reactivity down group 2 just as there is down group 1.

---

4 (a) (i) Correct plotting **2**
(5 points – 2 marks; 3–4 points – 1 mark)
Smooth curve (allow 1 for a curve which is not smooth) **2**

Examiner's tip Do not join points with straight lines or draw a thick line. A smooth curve is required.

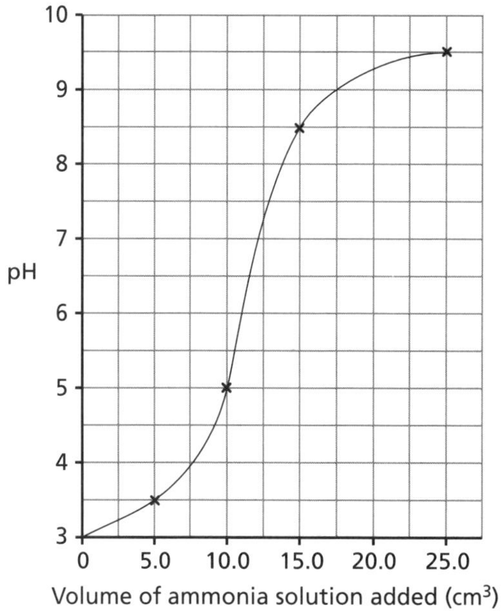

Question	Answer	Mark
(ii)	12 cm^3	1
(iii)	9.3–9.4	1
(iv)	When equal volumes of solutions are mixed the solution is alkaline	1
	Ammonia solution must therefore be more concentrated than the ethanoic acid solution	1
(b)	Water	1
	Alkali	1
	Salt	1
(c)	Pipette *or* burette	1

Examiner's tip You might be thinking of writing measuring cylinder. In fact this would be the best way of measuring out 20 cm^3 of solution, but it would not give the accuracy to measure out to the nearest 0.1 cm^3.

6 EXPLANATION OF THE PROPERTIES OF MATERIALS

Question	Answer	Mark
1 (a)	Gas	1

Examiner's tip Remember: there are three states of matter – solid, liquid and gas. Here in a gas the particles are widely spaced and moving rapidly.

Question	Answer	Mark
(b)	From left to right:	
	A compound – hydrogen bromide	1
	A mixture of hydrogen and bromine gases	1
	A mixture of hydrogen bromide, hydrogen and bromine	1

Examiner's tip This question is testing your understanding of elements, mixtures and compounds. In the molecules of the compound, atoms of hydrogen and bromine are combined. The third diagram is interesting. It represents either the situation during the reaction when the hydrogen and bromine molecules are being used up and hydrogen bromide molecules are forming *or* the system is in **equilibrium** when the rates of the forward and reverse reactions are equal. Candidates often are not clear about the distinction between elements, mixtures and compounds.

(c) (i)

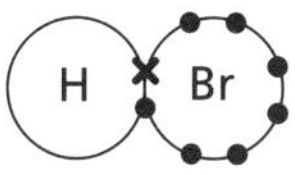

Question	Answer	Mark
(c) (i)	(diagram above)	2
	Covalent bonding	1
(ii)	Covalent bond broken	1
	Forms hydrogen ions and bromide ions	1
	H^+ and Br^-	1

Question	Answer	Mark
2 (a)	Particles in the gas are moving very rapidly *or* the movement has no pattern to it (i.e. random)	**1**
	Particles collide with the wall of the tyre creating pressure	**1**

Examiner's tip A very frequent mistake here is to explain the pressure of the gas by the collisions of the particles in the gas with each other.

(b)	When the car is used the temperature of the air in the tyre increases	**1**
	The particles in the air move faster and therefore make more collisions with the tyre wall	**1**

Examiner's tip A common incorrect answer here is to state that the increased temperature makes the particles expand and so the pressure goes up.

(c) (i)	Pressure, 200 kPa; volume, 1 dm^3	**1**

Examiner's tip The idea here is to get you to establish a pattern. As the pressure increases, the volume decreases. The pressure and volume are inversely proportional.

(ii)	Correct plotting of all points	**1**
	Smooth curve through the points	**1**

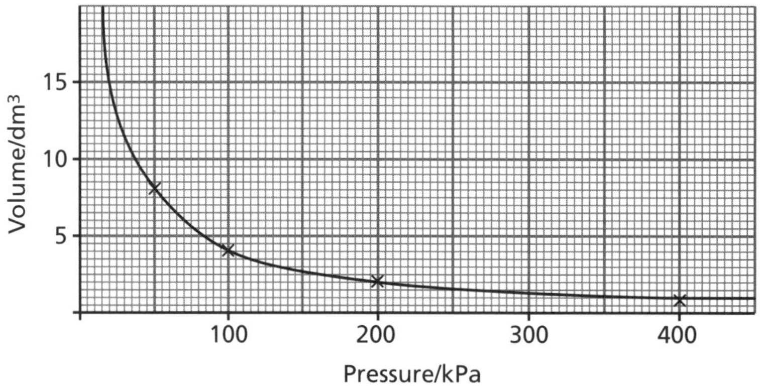

Examiner's tip You may have written the wrong values for pressure and volume in the table in (c)(i). You will still receive full marks for the graph if you correctly plotted these results and drew a good curve.

(iii)	$p_1V_1/T_1 = p_2V_2/T_2$ or $p_1/T_1 = p_2/T_2$ (as $V_1 = V_2$)	**1**
	Pressure $= 50 \times 400/300$	**1**
	$= 66.7$ kPa	**1**

Examiner's tip This question requires you to recall a formula (page 6). You will get 1 mark for doing this, 1 mark for substituting correctly in the formula and 1 mark for the correct answer with unit. Before moving on, check your answer is reasonable. You have increased the temperature, keeping the volume constant. It is reasonable for the pressure to have increased above 50 kPa. If you had an answer of 6.67 kPa because of an arithmetical mistake, you should realize it.

Question	Answer	Mark

Examiner's tip In this question the conditions are set up to ensure a 'fair test', e.g. drums of same shape and size, detector same distance from drum, etc. I assume that the radioactive waste is the same each time. There are only two variables – the material used for the drum and the thickness of the drum wall.

3	(a)	More radiation is absorbed by Nicad	**1**
		The thicker the alloy (Nicad or Zinctox) the more radiation is absorbed	**2**

Examiner's tip You are required to interpret the results in the table. The first conclusion can be obtained by comparing either the 1st and the 3rd set of results or the 2nd and the 4th. The second conclusion from the 1st and 2nd or 3rd and 4th.

	(b)	Possible reasons:	**2**
		To prevent them being accidentally dug up	
		So escaping radiation will be absorbed	
		So surface water is not contaminated	(any two)

4	(a)	A graph with a maximum as shown	**1**

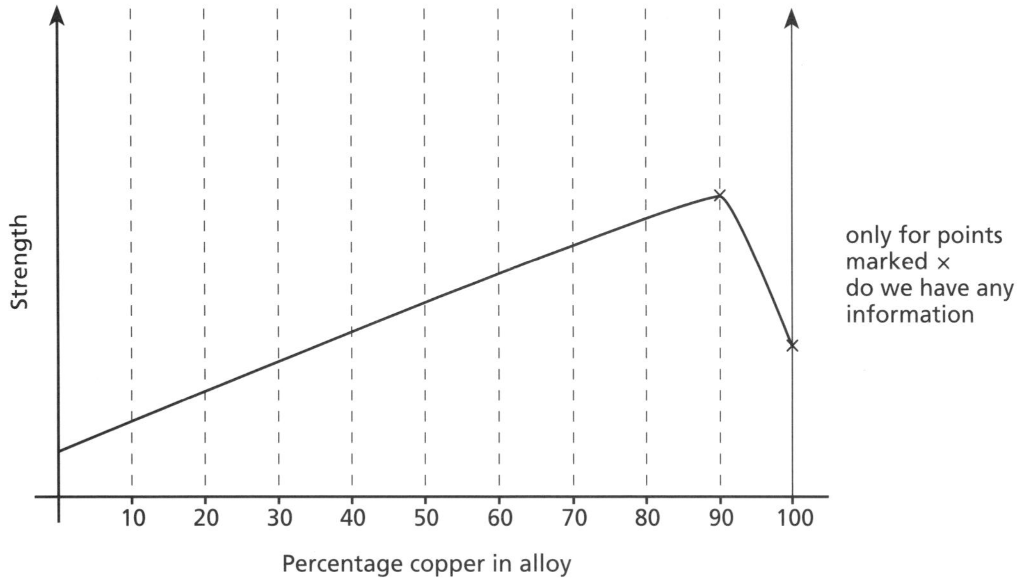

Examiner's tip You have little data to help you sketch the graph. The greatest strength of alloy contains 10% aluminium (or 90% copper) and this particular alloy has twice the strength of copper. The mark is for plotting the two points correctly and not for any line you draw.

	(b)	(i) The atoms of copper are closely packed	**1**
		Close packing of atoms produces a high density	**1**

Examiner's tip The high density of metals is due to close packing of atoms. Only the alkali metals, e.g. sodium and potassium, do not have this close packing and they have lower densities and float on water.

Question		Answer	Mark
	(ii)	The metal layers slide easily over one another	1
		There are no distortions (or dislocations) in the structure to prevent sliding	1
(c)	(i)	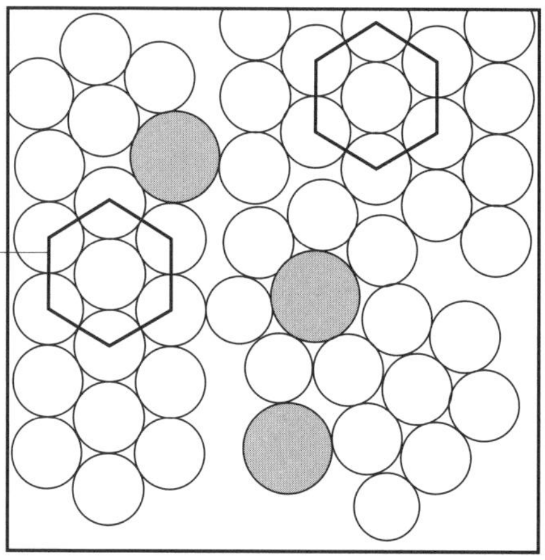	2

Examiner's tip Your diagram should show the regular structure of copper distorted by the presence of some aluminium atoms. Do not draw too many aluminium atoms. If you do it makes drawing the diagram more difficult.

	(ii)	The layers of atoms cannot slide over one another	1
		Irregularities in the structure prevent sliding	1
	(iii)	Aluminium bronze can be used for statues	1
		It is stronger than pure copper. It also retains the copper colour since it contains mainly copper	1

7 CHEMICAL CHANGES

Question		Answer	Mark
1	(a)	Natural gas	1
	(b)	Exothermic reaction	1
	(c)	Oxidation	1

Examiner's tip This is an oxidation reaction because hydrogen is lost when CH_3OH is converted into HCHO

	(d)	Large surface area for reaction to take place	1
	(e)	$CO(g) + 2H_2(g) \rightarrow CH_3OH(g)$	2

Examiner's tip 1 mark is awarded for getting the correct formulae for carbon monoxide, hydrogen and methanol in the correct place and the second mark is for balancing the equation. The state symbols are not necessary but, if you use them, you will not be penalized for a mistake. Note that methanol, which is a liquid at room temperature, is a gas at 300 °C.

Question	Answer	Mark
(f)	Either as a material for making polymers or for synthetic petrol	1

Examiner's tip In New Zealand, where there are supplies of natural gas but not petroleum, these processes are used to make synthetic petrol.

Question	Answer	Mark
2 (a) (i)	$Al^{3+} + 3e^- \rightarrow Al$	1
(ii)	1 mole of Al_2O_3 produces 2 moles Al	
	or 54 + 48 = 102 g Al_2O_3 produces 54 g Al	1
	500 kg Al produced by 500 × 102/54	1
	= 944.4 kg of aluminium oxide	1

Examiner's tip You could approximate the answer to 944 kg. Do not forget the unit.

Question	Answer	Mark
(b)	Six possible answers are:	4 (Two marks for each possibility. You need to give two.)
	High transport costs for ore: plant needs to be near a port	
	Cheap or plentiful supply of electricity needed: e.g. hydroelectric or nuclear power station	
	Fumes produced by plant: plant needs to be downwind of towns	
	Transport to and from the plant needed: close to motorway network	
	Transport will be noisy: plant needs to be away from residential areas	
	Good markets for aluminium: close to factories using aluminium	
(c)	Pb^{2+} rather than Al^{3+}	1
	Charge required is proportional to charge on ion	1

Question	Answer	Mark
3 (a)	The reaction has finished when all the acid is used up. From the graph, the reaction is complete after 6 minutes and the final volume of carbon dioxide formed is $58 cm^3$	2

Examiner's tip Check graph scales carefully. It is easy to give an answer of $59 cm^3$ or $54 cm^3$. Do not forget units.

Question	Answer	Mark
(b)	0–2 minutes	1
	The graph is steepest when the greatest volume of gas per minute is being produced	1

(c)

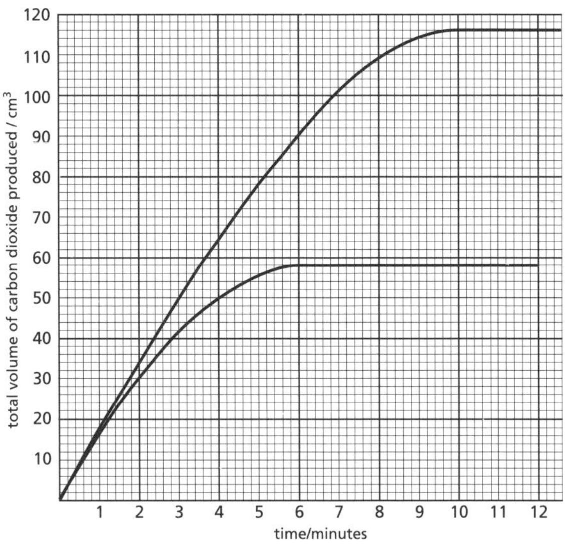

2

Question Answer Mark

> **Examiner's tip** You are not expected to draw an accurate graph, but only to sketch a graph. Your graph should be initially the same steepness as the original graph, but it should reach a maximum when twice the volume of gas is collected.

(d) (i) Reaction occurs when particles in the acid collide with the lump of marble **1**
Increasing the concentration of acid increases the number of particles in the acid and increases the number of collisions **1**
(ii) Increasing the temperature speeds up the particles in the acid **1**
Increasing the number of collisions of acid particles with the marble/more successful conditions **1**
(iii) Breaking up the marble increases its surface area **1**
So more chance of acid particles colliding with marble surface **1**

> **Examiner's tip** Explaining rate of reaction experiments in terms of collisions of particles is a common type of question on Higher GCSE papers.

(e) Mass of 1 mole of calcium carbonate = 40 + 12 + (3 x 16) = 100 g **1**
Mass of carbon dioxide formed by 1 mole of CaCO3
= 12 + (2 x 16) = 44 g **1**
5 g of $CaCO_3$ produces $\frac{44}{100} \times 5$ = 2.2 g of carbon dioxide **1**

---

4 (a) Energy is required to break existing bonds **1**
Energy is given out when new bonds are formed **1**
If the reaction is exothermic, the energy given out when new bonds form is greater than the energy required to break existing bonds **1**

> **Examiner's tip** A frequent problem seen on papers is that candidates get it the wrong way round and state that energy is given out when bonds are broken. This serious error leads to a loss of 3 marks straight away and has implications later in the question.

(b)

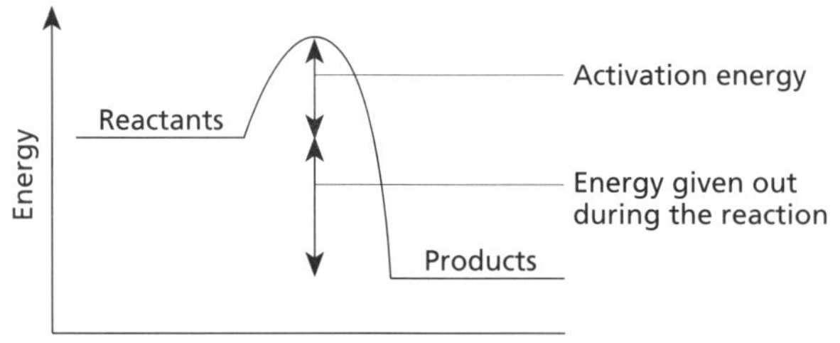

3

> **Examiner's tip** 1 mark is given for the energy of reactants being greater than that of products. 1 mark for reactants and products labelled. 1 mark for showing the energy given out. I have marked the activation energy on this diagram. It is not going to give me a mark at this stage, but will help me in my answer to (c).

(c) The activation energy is the energy reactants require to start the reaction **1**
Burning magnesium is an exothermic reaction **1**
This energy starts the Thermit reaction. Once underway the reaction continues because the reaction is exothermic **1**
(d) There is a variety of acceptable answers, including:
Heat resistant clothing and gloves to resist high temperatures
Dust masks, as metal powders can be toxic **2**

8 THE EARTH AND ITS ATMOSPHERE

Question		Answer	Mark
1 (a)		Average density of the Earth is greater than densities of crustal and mantle rocks	1
		There must be very high density material within the Earth, i.e. core	1
(b)	(i)	S_3	1
		Does not receive S waves as there is liquid within the Earth that these will not pass through	1
	(ii)	S_1	1
		Closer to the source of the earthquake	1
(c)	(i)	Iceland is at the junction of two plates	1
		At this point the plates are moving apart	1
		New rock being formed by crystallization of magma will be igneous	1
	(ii)	African and Eurasian plates are moving towards each other. Rocks are pushed upwards	1
		One plate moves over the other and the lower plate returns to the magma	1

Examiner's tip
The movement of plates continues today. However, erosion of the mountains counteracts the tendency for the Himalayas to become higher.

Question	Answer	Mark
2 (a)	*You have to choose suitable scales before you plot the points. You should try to fill the graph paper.*	
	Suitable scales – on the y axis 200 or 250 to 2 cm	
	– on the x axis 10 to 2 cm	1
	Axes labelled with name and unit	1
	Correct plotting	1
	Straight line	1

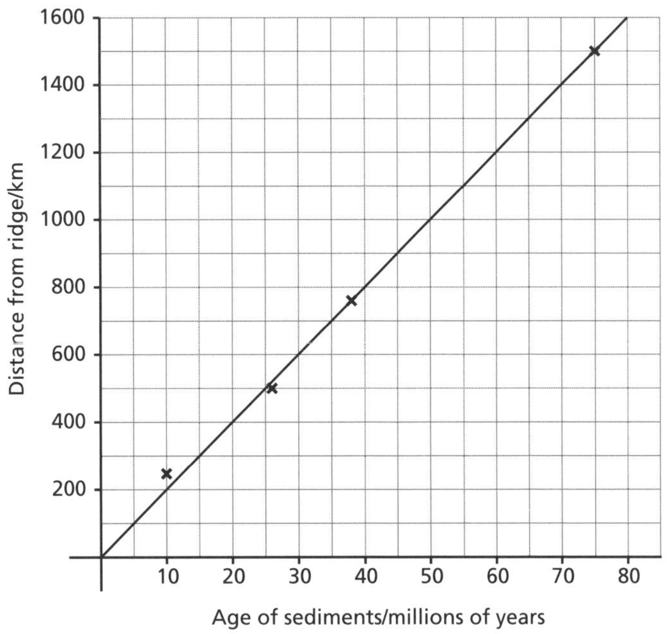

Question		Answer	Mark

> **Examiner's tip** Do not join the points with straight lines. Remember there will be some possibility of error in these results. Also continue your graph back to zero. When the age is zero, the distance moved will be zero.

Question		Answer	Mark
(b)	(i)	To find the rate of spreading find the gradient (steepness) of the graph by dividing distance by time e.g. 950/50 = 19 km/million years	1

> **Examiner's tip** This graph you have drawn is a distance–time graph.

Question		Answer	Mark
	(ii)	From your graph you should have a reading of approximately 50 million years	1
(c)		Convection currents in the magma	1
		Bring rocks to the surface	1
		Lava or magma escapes through cracks or pressure forces lava or magma up	1
		Constructive plate boundary	1
(d)		Less carbon dioxide when there is no volcanic activity so less photosynthesis takes place	1
		Less oxygen *or* less food *or* global cooling	1

9 ELECTRICITY AND MAGNETISM

Question		Answer	Mark
1 (a)		Any warm object such as a person or a car engine	1
(b)	(i)	0	1
		0	1
		1	1
		0	1

> **Examiner's tip** Both inputs have to be '1' for the output of an AND gate to be '1'.

Question		Answer	Mark
	(ii)	It must be dark	1
		And there must be a warm object to cause the infrared to be 'high'	1
(c)	(i)	The lamp goes off when he drives the car into the garage	1
	(ii)	A bistable latch could be placed between the AND gate and the relay	1
		This would keep the lamp switched on	1
		After the output from the AND gate had changed to 0	1

> **Examiner's tip** You should also remember that a bistable latch needs to have a means of resetting it.

Question			Answer	Mark
2	(a)	(i)	The circuit allows the brightness of the lamp to be changed	1

Examiner's tip Answers such as 'make the lamp dimmer' or 'make the lamp brighter' would be acceptable.

		(ii)	Resistance	1
			Greatest	1
			Current	1
			Smallest	1

Examiner's tip Resistance measures the opposition to current; the more resistance in a circuit, the less current passes.

	(b)	(i)	Knowledge of formula $R = V \div I$	1
			$= 12\,V \div 0.2\,A$	1
			$= 60\,\Omega$	1

Examiner's tip In any calculation, always write down the formula that you are using. This helps to prevent errors that can easily happen when you are in an examination. Also, take care to make sure that you give the correct unit with the answer.

		(ii)	Knowledge of formula $P = V \times I$	1
			$= 12\,V \times 0.2\,A$	1
			$= 2.4\,W$	1

---

3 (a) The completed diagram should look like:

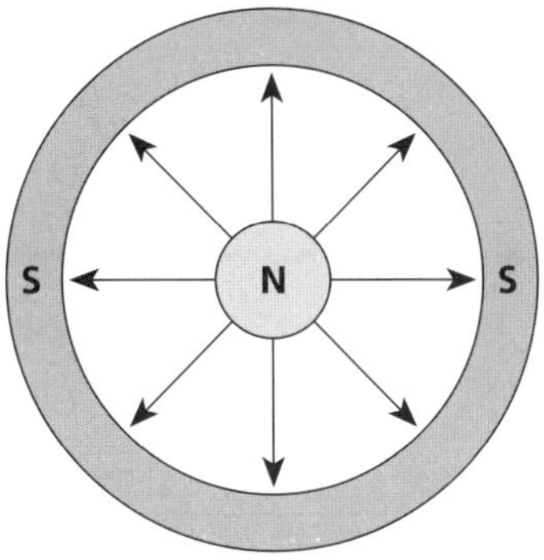

			The field lines are radial	1
			With arrows pointing from N to S	1

Examiner's tip The direction of a magnetic field is the direction of the force on the N pole of a magnet.

	(b)		The paper cone vibrates	1
			This vibration is horizontal *or* an in and out movement	1
			When a current passes, its magnetic field causes movement	1

Question			Answer	Mark
			When the direction of the current changes, the direction of the movement changes	1

Examiner's tip The first 2 marks are for 'describe' and the last 2 for 'explain'. You must remember to do both.

Question			Answer	Mark
	(c)		Electrical energy from the amplifier	1
			Is transferred to energy of the free electrons	1
			This is transferred to the cone as the current passes through the coil	1

Examiner's tip In any circuit, the charge carriers are the 'go-betweens'; they transfer the energy from the source to the components.

Question			Answer	Mark
4	(a)	(i)	power = current × potential difference or $P = I \times V$	1
		(ii)	power = $6\ V \times 0.3\ A$	1
			$= 1.8\ W$	1
	(b)		A voltage is produced in the secondary coil when the magnetic field from the primary coil changes	1
			With a steady direct current in the primary, the magnetic field does not change	1

Examiner's tip When answering questions on electromagnetic induction, you should emphasize the changing magnetic field.

Question			Answer	Mark
	(c)		The output voltage is 1/40 of the input	1
			So the secondary coil has 1/40 the number of turns of the primary	1
			Which is $8000 \div 40 = 200$	1

Examiner's tip The transformer equation (see p55) could be used to give the same result, but it is usually easier to use the turns ratio directly.

10 ENERGY RESOURCES AND ENERGY TRANSFER

Question		Answer	Mark
1	(a)	Chemical	1
		Kinetic	1
	(b)	Gravitational potential	1
		Kinetic	1
	(c)	Electrical	1
		Sound	1
	(d)	Chemical	1
		Thermal	1

Question	Answer	Mark
2 (a)	Hydroelectric power is renewable; it does not use up any of the Earth's energy resources	**1**
	It does not produce carbon dioxide or other greenhouse gases	**1**
	It does not leave ash or produce sulphur dioxide	**1**

Examiner's tip Many candidates confuse the effects of pollution caused by emission of gases into the atmosphere. Carbon dioxide, water vapour and methane all contribute to the greenhouse effect and sulphur dioxide contributes towards acid rain.

Question	Answer	Mark
(b)	The Sun	**1**

Examiner's tip The Sun provides the majority of the Earth's energy sources.

Question	Answer	Mark
(c) (i)	Gravitational potential energy in the water	**1**
	Changes to kinetic energy as the water falls	**1**
	This is transferred to electrical energy in the generators	**1**
(ii)	Knowledge of formula change in gpe $= m \times g \times \Delta h$	**1**
	$= 2.5 \times 10^5 \times 10 \times 190$	**1**
	$= 4.75 \times 10^8\,\text{J}$	**1**
(iii)	Max power output = 60% × power input	**1**
	$= 0.6 \times 4.75 \times 10^8\,\text{J/s}$	**1**
	$= 2.85 \times 10^8\,\text{W}$	**1**
(iv)	Not all the kinetic energy can be removed from the water; it has to have some movement when it leaves the generators	**2**
(v)	Any two answers from:	
	Pumped storage stations can be brought into operation very rapidly	
	They 'use' energy at night when it is readily available	
	They do not cause any atmospheric pollution	**2** (1 mark each)

Question	Answer	Mark
3 (a)	Knowledge of formula work = force × distance moved in direction of force $= Fs$	**1**
	= 4000 N × 1.8 m	**1**
	= 7200 J	**1**
(b)	Work = 2200 N × 3.6 m	**1**
	= 7920 J	**1**
(c)	More work has to be done when dragging because of friction forces	**1**
	The extra energy is transferred to thermal energy	**1**
	The thermal energy is in the ramp and the load	**1**

Examiner's tip Whenever two surfaces rub against each other some work has to be done against the friction forces that oppose the motion; this causes heating of the surfaces that are rubbing.

Question	Answer	Mark
(d)	The ramp enables a smaller force to be used	**1**

Question			Answer	Mark
4	(a)	(i)	Knowledge of formula	
			Energy = mass × specific heat capacity × temperature change = $mc\Delta T$	1
			= 85 kg × 1200 J/kg °C × 180 °C	1
			= 18.36 MJ	1
			(1 MJ = 1 × 10⁶ J)	
		(ii)	The casing also has to be heated up	1
	(b)		Energy is transferred by conduction	1
			In conduction the energy travels through the concrete blocks and the casing to the air	1
			Energy is transferred by convection	1
			The air around the heater is warmed, rises and is replaced by colder air	1
			Energy is transferred by radiation	1
			The warm casing emits electromagnetic radiation	1

Examiner's tip Transfer of thermal energy is always by a combination of conduction, convection and radiation. When answering questions about thermal energy transfer, give some detail as well as naming the way in which energy is transferred.

	(c)	(i)	The energy from the heater replaces energy which is being lost from the room	1
			This energy is lost through the walls, windows, floor and ceiling	1
			It ends up spread out in the surroundings	1
			The room temperature is constant because energy is being gained from the heater at the same rate as it is being lost to the outside	1
		(ii)	The energy from the heater raises the temperature of the surroundings by a small amount	1
			It is very difficult to recover energy from a low-temperature source	1

11 FORCES AND THEIR EFFECTS

Question		Answer	Mark
1	(a)	Two equal size arrows drawn	1
		One upwards and one downwards	1
		The upward force is the magnet's pull on the paperclip	1
		The downward force is the Earth's pull on the paperclip or the weight of the paperclip	1

Examiner's tip When describing forces, use the form 'object A pulls/pushes on object B'.

	(b)	The forces are equal in size	1
		Because the paperclip is not moving	1

Examiner's tip The forces acting on any object which is not moving or is moving in a straight line at a constant speed are balanced.

Question	Answer	Mark
(c)	The paperclip will move to the left	1
	The force from the left-hand magnet is bigger	1
	Because the paperclip is nearer to the left-hand magnet	1
2 (a) (i)	Knowledge of formula pressure = force ÷ area	1
	= 800 N ÷ 0.8 m^2	1
	= 1000 Pa	1

Examiner's tip The unit N/m^2 or N m^{-2} is an acceptable alternative to Pa.

Question	Answer	Mark
(ii)	The pressure is doubled	1
	Because the same force is acting	1
	On half the area	1
(b)	pressure = 500 N ÷ 0.0002 m^2	1
	= 2.5×10^6 Pa	1
3 (a)	The force in diagram B has the greater turning effect	1
	The perpendicular distance from the force line to the pivot is greater	1
(b)	Knowledge of formula	
	Moment = force × perpendicular distance to pivot	1
	= 200 N × 0.15 m	1
	= 30 N m	1
(c) (i)	Moment = 120 N × 0.3 m	1
	= 36 N m	1
(ii)	The braking will be less effective	1
	The distance from the force to the axis of rotation is smaller	1
	So the force from the brake has a smaller moment and is less effective in stopping the wheel from turning	1
(d) (i)	A speeding up or accelerating	1
	B travelling at a constant speed	1
	C speeding up or accelerating	1
	D slowing down to a halt	1
(ii)	Knowledge of formula distance travelled = speed × time	1
	= 8 m/s × 17 s	1
	= 136 m	1
(iii)	Knowledge of formula acceleration = increase in speed ÷ time taken	1
	= 8 m/s ÷ 9 s	1
	= 0.89 m/s^2	1
(iv)	Knowledge of formula force = mass × acceleration	1
	= 95 kg × 0.89 m/s^2	1
	= 84.4 N	1
(v)	As the cyclist goes faster the resistive forces increase	1
	This reduces the size of the unbalanced force and so the acceleration decreases	1

Question	Answer	Mark

Examiner's tip If the resistive forces have a value of 20 N this reduces the effective forwards force to 64.4 N.

(vi) Knowledge of formula kinetic energy $= \frac{1}{2} \times m \times v^2$ **1**
$= \frac{1}{2} \times 95 \times 12^2$ **1**
$= 6840$ J **1**

Examiner's tip When using the kinetic energy formula, don't forget that only the speed is squared, not the whole expression.

(vii) Knowledge of formula
Acceleration = increase in velocity ÷ time taken **1**
$= -12 \div 15 = -0.8\ \text{m/s}^2$ **1**

Examiner's tip The force is calculated using the formula force = mass × acceleration; first the acceleration has to be calculated, using the data from the graph. The minus sign shows that it is a deceleration and can be ignored.

Force = mass × acceleration **1**
= 95 × 0.8
= 76 N **1**

(viii) Knowledge of formula distance = average speed × time **1**
= 6 m/s × 15 s **1**
= 90 m **1**

(ix) Time taken to stop = 7.5 s **1**
Distance travelled = 3 m/s × 7.5 s **1**
= 22.5 m **1**

Examiner's tip For the same force, the time taken to stop from a speed of 6 m/s would be half that taken to stop from a speed of 12 m/s.

(x) Braking from 12 m/s takes twice as long as from 6 m/s **1**
And the average speed while braking is twice as much **1**
These factors combine to make the braking distance four times as great **1**

---

4 (a) Multiply the mass (1 mark) by the velocity (1 mark) **2**

(b) The total momentum before the collision **1**
Is equal to the total momentum after the collision **1**

Examiner's tip The word 'total' is important here; it is the sum of the momentum of each object, taking into account the directions.

(c) (i) Momentum before the collision = 2 kg × 6 m/s **1**
= 12 Ns **1**

Examiner's tip An alternative unit for momentum is kgm/s or kgms^{-1}.

Question	Answer	Mark
	Speed after the collision = momentum ÷ mass	1
	= 12Ns ÷ 3 kg = 4 m/s	1

Examiner's tip Although the momentum is the same, the total moving mass has increased, causing a reduction in velocity.

Question	Answer	Mark
(ii)	Kinetic energy = $^1/_2$mv2	1
	Before the collision, ke = $^1/_2 \times 2 \times 6^2$ = 36 J	1
	After the collision, ke = $^1/_2 \times 3 \times 4^2$ = 24 J	1
	Loss in ke is 12 J	1

Examiner's tip Whenever objects collide, some kinetic energy is transferred to heat. Unlike momentum, kinetic energy is not conserved in collisions.

12 LIGHT AND SOUND

Question	Answer	Mark
1 (a) (i)	The prongs vibrate or oscillate	1
	They complete 256 vibrations each second	1
(ii)	It is a higher pitch	1
(iii)	Knowledge of formula wavelength = speed ÷ frequency	1
	= 330 m/s v 256 Hz	1
	= 1.29 m	1
(b) (i)	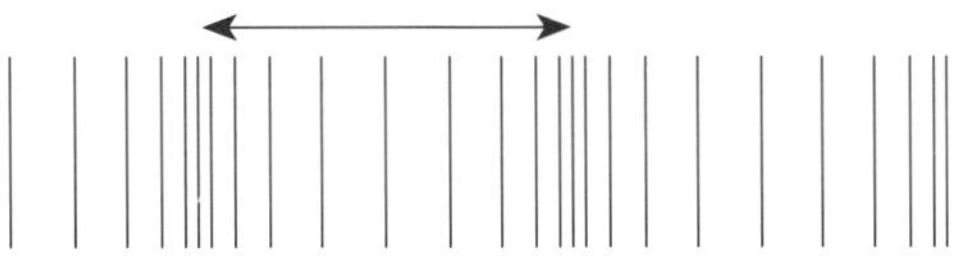	1

Examiner's tip Your arrow should show a compression and a rarefaction; an easy way of doing this is to draw an arrow from the centre of one compression to the centre of the next one. Another way is to draw an arrow from the centre of one rarefaction to the centre of the next.

Question	Answer	Mark
(ii)	The air molecules vibrate or oscillate	1
	Along the direction in which the wave is travelling	1

Examiner's tip It is important to specify the direction precisely when you are describing a wave motion.

Question	Answer	Mark
(iii)	They vibrate with a bigger amplitude	1
	But the number of vibrations each second remains the same	1
(c)	All objects have a natural frequency of vibration	1
	All objects vibrate when sound waves hit them	1
	If the frequency of the sound waves is the same as the natural frequency of vibration, then large amplitude vibrations can build up	1

Question			Answer	Mark
2	(a)	(i)	Light from the Sun is reflected by the tree	1
		(ii)	Your diagram should show light from the tree being reflected at the water surface so that the angle of incidence is equal to the angle of reflection	1
		(iii)	The image should be:	
			Directly below the tree, each point being the same distance below the level of the water surface as the actual tree is above it	1
			Upside down	1
			The same size as the tree	1
		(iv)	The image is a virtual one	1
			Light appears to have come from the image, but it has not really come from there	1
	(b)		This is what the completed diagrams should look like:	

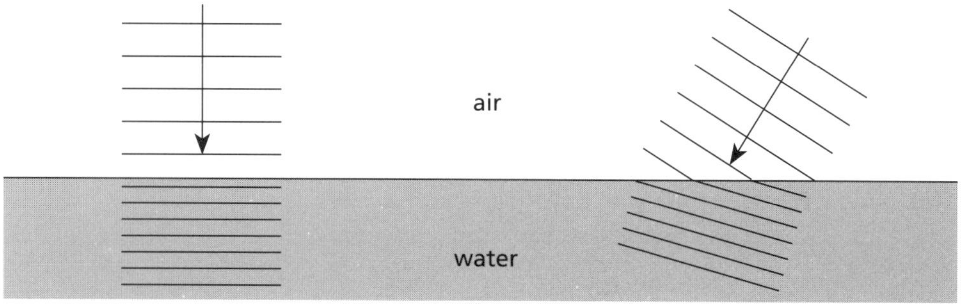

			The marks are for:	
			Left-hand diagram: reduced wavelength	1
			no change in direction	1
			Right-hand diagram: reduced wavelength	1
			correct change in direction	1
	(c)		Your diagrams should show the oscillations restricted to one direction in each case	1

			1 mark for showing the oscillations and direction of travel in each diagram	2
	(d)		Much of the light reflected from the water surface is horizontally polarized	1
			This light does not pass through the Polaroid	1
			Vertical oscillations are the only ones that do pass through	1

Examiner's tip All these points could have been shown on a 'before and after' diagram.

3	(a)		Knowledge of formula wavelength = speed ÷ frequency	1
			$= 3.0 \times 10^8\,\text{m/s} \div 1.0 \times 10^8\,\text{Hz}$	1
			$= 3.0\,\text{m}$	1

Question	Answer	Mark
(b)	1×10^8 Hz is at or close to the natural frequency of oscillation	1
	This causes a large-amplitude vibration	1
	1×10^6 Hz is not close to the natural frequency and only causes a small-amplitude vibration	1

Examiner's tip If you missed the last point you have not answered the last part of the question. Take care to answer all of the question, and not just a part of it.

Question	Answer	Mark
(c) (i)	A narrow beam can locate a target more precisely than a wide beam can	1
(ii)	The waves are diffracted (spread out) when they leave the reflector	1
	The diameter of the reflector needs to be many times the wavelength to reduce this spreading	1

Examiner's tip When answering questions about diffraction, you should always make a comparison between the wavelength and the size of the aperture where the diffraction is taking place.

Question	Answer	Mark
(iii)	Your diagram should show the waves spreading out	1
	The spread should be through 180°	1

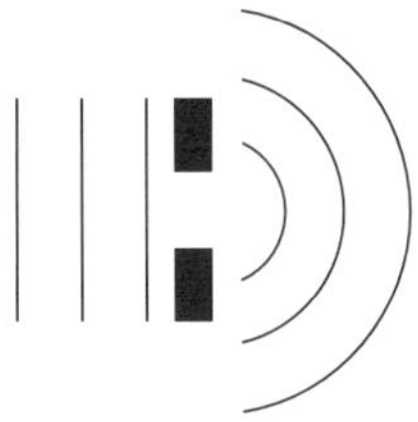

13 THE EARTH'S PLACE IN THE UNIVERSE

Question	Answer	Mark
1 (a)	Venus has a circular orbit, so it is a constant distance from the Sun	1
	Mercury's orbit is elliptical, so its distance from the Sun varies	1
(b)	As Mercury gets nearer to the Sun it speeds up	1
	Because the gravitational pull of the Sun is increasing	1
	As it moves further away from the Sun it slows down	1
	Because the gravitational pull of the Sun is decreasing	1
(c)	Venus travels slower in its orbit than Mercury does	1
	It also has further to travel to complete an orbit	1
(d)	They all have similar densities	1
(e)	The Earth and Venus both have atmospheres	1
	They also both have clouds	1
	Wind and rain would have eroded craters	1
(f)	The atmosphere is acidic and very corrosive	1
	It is also likely to be very hot	1

Examiner's tip Venus is closer to the Sun than the Earth, so it receives more radiation on each square metre. The carbon dioxide atmosphere will help to keep the planet hot, as a result of the greenhouse effect.

Question		Answer	Mark
2	(a)	Hydrogen and helium nuclei were forced together at high speeds	1
		They fused to form the nuclei of heavier elements	1
	(b)	The Earth is rich in elements that are heavier than hydrogen and helium	1
		These did not exist when the first stars formed	1
	(c)	The lighter materials would have moved to the outside of the spinning cloud	1
		Leaving the heavier materials on the inside	1
	(d)	All the objects in the Universe attract each other	1
		This gravitational force is slowing down the rate of expansion	1
	(e)	The path of the galaxies can be traced back	1
		They appear to have started from a common point in space	1
3	(a)	Your arrow should go from the Moon towards the centre of the Earth	1
	(b)	The water on the side facing the Moon experiences the strongest gravitational pull and so the water is deeper here	1
		The water on the side away from the Moon is less affected by the gravitational pull and so it has not been pulled towards the Moon	1
	(c)	The Earth rotates on its own axis once each day	1
		So different parts of the Earth pass through the water bulges	1
		In one day each point on the Earth's surface goes through a cycle of two lots of shallow water and two lots of deep water	1

Examiner's tip Because of the Moon's rotation about the Earth, the cycle takes slightly longer than one day to complete.

Question		Answer	Mark
	(d)	They should analyse the rocks to discover the chemical make-up	1
		They should look for evidence of volcanic activity	1